UNSTOPPABLE
STORIES

COMPILED BY
GERALDINE McGRATH
AWARD-WINNING PODCAST HOST

KMD
BOOKS

First published in Australia in 2024
by KMD Books
Waikiki, WA 6169

Typeset in Adobe Garamond Pro 12.5/18pt

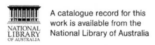 A catalogue record for this
work is available from the
National Library of Australia

National Library of Australia Catalogue-in-Publication data:

Unstoppable Stories/Geraldine McGrath

ISBN:
978-0-9942105-3-1
(Paperback)

DEDICATION

*U*nstoppable Stories* is dedicated to the remarkable women who have made this impactful creation possible. My heartfelt thanks extend to all the incredible individuals who have supported me on this journey. To my children, Craig, Kristen, Courtney, Kiana and our angel baby; to my husband Declan; to my parents; to my sisters and all my family; to my friends and mentors, I am truly beyond grateful.

A special word of dedication is reserved for the late Natalia, whose life was tragically taken by homicide. Her sister, Magdalena, has honoured her with a chapter in this book.

To women worldwide enduring domestic abuse, I hope this book reaches you and brings strength, hope and resilience for the journey ahead. A chapter dedicated to you has been written by Lejla Dauti, founder of Lejla Please Tell My Story.

Royalties from *Unstoppable Stories* will be dedicated to suicide prevention work, creating 'an unstoppable movement' to break down the stigma and silence associated with it.

Thank you all for being a part of my life. I am blessed beyond words.

ACKNOWLEDGMENTS

The journey of creating "Unstoppable Stories" has been nothing short of extraordinary, from its initial spark of inspiration to its release into the world. Embracing an inspired vision and pursuing it with heart-felt dedication has created a magic of profound purpose.

I extend my heartfelt gratitude to each author of "Unstoppable Stories." Your faith in this journey and your commitment have united into a potent, heart-driven force, becoming truly unstoppable. My sincere thanks to every one of you.

Special acknowledgment to our celebrity guests, Laurie Burrows and Jaque Almeida, for imparting your wisdom and helping to amplify this powerful work.

Immense thanks to Karen and the entire team at KMD Books for their guidance and support. To Frankie, whose artistic talent has gifted our book with its distinctive and engaging design, a heartfelt thank you. Gratitude also to anyone who has contributed in any way with Unstoppable Stories.

Heartfelt thanks to you, the reader, for welcoming this book into your life.

With love & gratitude, Geraldine xx

unstoppable[1]
(ʌnstɒpəbəl IPA Pronunciation Guide)

ADJECTIVE
Something that is unstoppable cannot be prevented from continuing
or developing.

1   https://www.collinsdictionary.com/dictionary/english/unstoppable

"Unstoppable: Where Grit Meets Inner Fulfilment and Compassion, Shaping Barriers into Bridges."

GERALDINE MCGRATH

AWARD-WINNING PODCAST HOST OF RADIATE REALNESS

CONTENTS

FOREWORD
KAREN WEAVER

Stories break down barriers and facilitate a sacred space for conversations to be held. Conversations that have the potential to heal, connect, ignite and even change a life. When someone reads a story that they are destined to read they will never go back from that moment, it will propel them forward in the knowing they are not alone and in the hope that there is light at the end of the tunnel.

Each story in *Unstoppable Stories* will be that for a reader and there is no greater gift in the world to give than sharing your story of triumph through adversity because in that choice the author relinquishes shame and stands in the power that is their story so that others can benefit. Each one of the authors in this book are the heroines of their story.

It is an honour to have been asked to write the foreword for this book. Geraldine's strong vision and courage to lead each of these carefully chosen women through the process of writing and sharing their stories is commendable. I have been delighted to have been part of the process not only as the publisher but in joining this passionate leader on this journey.

As a reader, you are in for a treat in the pages of this book. It is powerful so be prepared to feel all the feels and be inspired to act in your own life or maybe share this book with someone you know needs to read it.

KAREN WEAVER

Congratulations to all the UNSTOPPABLE authors in *Unstoppable Stories!*

CELEBRITY GUEST
LAURIE BURROWS

From a young age, I always knew I wanted to run my own business. My parents divorced when I was eight years old, and though it's a story I don't overly share, reflection has made me realise how relevant it is to everything that happened next, as I was able to observe two very different lifestyles. My dad could buy whatever he wanted, whenever he wanted. He wasn't super wealthy, but he had a good job and never really thought twice about spending money. On the flip side, mum's lifestyle was essentially that she lived in poverty. We had to ration shampoo and share towels to save on washing - that kind of poor.

These observations made me realise I wanted more. I wanted to be like my dad, so I became very entrepreneurial from a young age. I remember exploring Google at 11-years-old, to find how I could get into college early or take an evening class that would enable me to *start my career*. This was before the era of online education and YouTube that we have access to these days, and of course, nowhere was going to take an eleven-year-old into their night class or college. So instead, I started a cleaning business. I began by cleaning family homes, just to make some money. My first job was my dad's house, cleaning it every Saturday for £5; this eventually became £10 and then £15 and so on. I found it exciting to be making money and that led me to learn more skills, as well as discover how I could monetise those skills.

I started my first eBay business selling jewellery. It only stopped because I was kicked off the site – all sellers were required to be 18, and because I was selling so much, they asked for ID, discovering I was only 16. Despite the setback, I had saved enough for my first overseas holiday.

I continued on my entrepreneurial journey, starting several businesses that weren't always super successful, but one that helped me progress was charging £5 for doing a set of nails; essentially £5 per hour, if that. Doing nails led me at the age of eighteen, to start a little drop-shipping business selling hair extensions. Eventually I learned how to do hair extensions, which helped me make more money. By this time, I was at university studying for my business degree, and during my studies, I would get as much work-experience as I could handle, because well, I just wanted to learn *more*.

Work experience meant spending my time in marketing and business management, and I think it's important to note, the reason I'm so good at what I do and why I've supported so many people in quitting their jobs and starting successful businesses, is because of my very strong work ethic. From eleven years old, I was always out there, learning and educating myself, getting tonnes of work experience during university with different brands and different companies, supporting them with their marketing. I also learnt a lot outside of university too. I wasn't just studying my degree; I was taking extra courses, learning and developing, wanting to become the best of the best.

When I left university, I was immediately offered a good job as a marketing manager. At just 22 I went on to become a trainer and mentor for probably the largest apprenticeship company in the UK at the time. It's quite a story, as I was their youngest trainer and assessor, teaching level three and level four apprentices; 16-20-year-olds just a couple of years younger than me. However, my experience was vastly different, with all the work I'd done from the age of 11.

By 24, I was promoted to *regional lead* in my subject of **digital marketing**. My responsibility was to oversee three colleges, as well as the assessors and trainers. I was then offered an opportunity to oversee all their marketing.

I took the position as head of marketing, which eventually led to me starting my own business. Initially working out of my bedroom, juggling business strategies and baby bottles, I grew from startup to making 7 figures in revenue in my business.

MY RELATIONSHIPS

Something I've rarely openly shared, was that at the age of 18, I was in a very toxic and abusive relationship; specifically, emotional abuse. Despite all my successes in other areas of my life, this relationship led me to attempt suicide at 18, and again when I was about 20.

I believe what I saw in relationships around me as I grew up, led to me accepting being in such a toxic relationship. I fell into the trap myself, which led me to hurting myself because of it.

Between the ages of 15 to 18, I was in a good relationship and we moved in together at 17, after I had an argument with my dad. I left him at 18 though because I was growing up and realised he'd become a whole new person.

I quickly met another guy in his mid-twenties, and thought I was head over heels, utterly in love - but it was a very controlling relationship. I couldn't have any friends, especially male friends, and he'd check my phone constantly. Even after the first six weeks and our first argument, I had completely lost my self-worth and my self-love.

I developed major body dysmorphia; At 7 stone ... I thought I was 27 stone, always looking in the mirror at myself. The abuse played with my mindset. Most 18-year-olds going to university were living in uni-accommodation, but I had my own little place. He moved in with me so he could control me. When we argued, the emotional abuse would send me spiralling into self-loathing. After a time, it also turned into physical abuse.

The first time I tried to commit suicide, I ended up in hospital. Despite everything, I went back with him. I stayed with him for three years, though we did have a few breaks in between, but he always made me feel so tiny, so dumb - *so worthless.* At 20, I didn't know how to get out of the situation. I hated being with him, I was constantly depressed, but I didn't tell anyone – no one knew what I was going through …. except my housemate.

She found me on the floor after I'd taken an overdose. She got me to hospital and saved my life. Since then, after I left him, I've been focusing on my mental health, slowly working on myself. Though I still ended up in a couple of toxic relationships … they didn't last long.

Despite all that happened, and what I was happening in my personal life, my career was almost polar opposite; my working and professional life was flourishing. It was almost as if what was happening behind the scenes was fuelling it - I had to have something good in my life.

All my good career choices led to starting my business … and that's then when I got pregnant after six weeks of meeting a guy. Yeah, we got married …. and of course, now we're getting divorced!

MY HEALTH

I was that annoying kid who got all the best grades in the class, despite a lack of attendance. I nearly got kicked out of college and university because my attendance was so shockingly bad. I preferred to study at home. I'd read from a book and learn what I needed to pass all my tests and exams. But the main reason for my lack of attendance, was because I would fall asleep in class. I later found out I had a chronic disease syndrome which meant I would fall asleep … anywhere, anytime. It also continued when I was working, so being my own boss and working in my own time is essential for me.

It wasn't just falling asleep that was the problem, I was also getting headaches and other symptoms. I was eventually diagnosed, but never got any medical help around it, mainly because I couldn't get myself to the necessary appointments. Having moved out on my own at 17, I was struggling financially. The doctors wanted me to go to a hospital appointment in Norfolk, a long bus journey away. On the day, I didn't have the money to get there, and had no-one I could ask for help. Over time, I learnt to work with my fatigue syndrome, teaching myself coping strategies, to complete my studies and get through my day's work, despite regularly falling asleep.

LOSS

My dad suffered from a rare brain condition called CJD. It was picked up when he started acting strangely during COVID. He would say he could see things in his house, like monkeys and bugs. At first, we thought it was dementia, but later discovered it was CJD and he was only given six months to live. He managed to hold on a little longer; long enough to meet my little boy, which was amazing. A couple of months after losing dad, my nan also passed away unexpectedly. With my dad, I had time to prepare, but with Nan, she had a heart attack and was gone. It was really tough because I was so close to her.

I very nearly missed seeing her for the last time, because my son had been unsettled the night before and I called and asked if I could take her for a meal on Monday instead of seeing her that day. "No," she said. "Please come and see me today. I really want to see you ... today." I'm so grateful I did, because that was the last day I saw her.

Part of me thinks she knew, because the conversation we had that day was strange.

THE BUSINESS JOURNEY

Like many things in life, the business journey has been a little rocky.

Initially I did well. My first official year in business was in 2019, but I treated it like a hobby, not really taking it seriously. In 2020, when I did take it seriously, I realised, *I can actually make something of this.* That was the month I found out I was pregnant, but it didn't deter me, it strengthened me. I had to look closely at my business goals, as I'd started my business because I wanted to make more money.

I wanted to make five grand a month working less … and I did that.

That year I made $185,000 through digital marketing platform - *KAJABI.* It was an incredible first year. Of course, there's been ups and downs since, as business is not an easy ride. We see plenty of stuff on social media that lures us into thinking it will be easy, but challenges are all part of the journey, so we have to embrace them and keep going. Some months aren't as good as others. We've had failed launches and we've had to get rid of team members. Things go wrong all the time, but they also go right, so I have learned to embrace it all.

My story is filled with extremes, but everything has led me to starting this business and becoming a mum; two things I was destined to do.

What is important for us all, is to be aware of and focus on our mental health. When I started my business, I was still very much affected by the trauma and abuse I had experienced through my childhood. I guess I thought that making money, and having a successful business would make up for the pain. However, that is not the case and what is most important, is dealing with the trauma. For many years, despite having a great career and successful business, I was absolutely miserable. Although I had been working on my mindset to achieve so much, I wasn't focussing on my mental health and finding ways to heal everything I'd been through. I was chasing money, thinking it would make me feel good. Over the last year or so, I have discovered I'm focussing on my healing journey. This has made me realise what I actually want in life. It's not about the money, it's about feeling happy within myself. Through the adversity, I have continued to grow my business and myself. I am proud of what I've achieved professionally, but even prouder of developing the understanding that mental health and inner happiness comes first. My advice … work through your trauma and abuse – it's the only way to truly heal.

LAURIE BURROWS

Growing up, Laurie lived with very little. She recalls having to ration shampoo as a child because they couldn't afford to buy more. Living on benefits and learning how to go without shaped the person she is today.

After so many years with not very much, Laurie decided something had to change. She needed to create a life where she no longer worried about how to put food on the table or pay the rent.

That's why, at the age of 18, she began to launch business after business on her own.

At first, she would always end up going back into corporate work. By the age of 23 she was a Lead Digital Marketing Mentor, creating courses and programs which were rolled out across 36 colleges around the UK. By 24, Laurie was Head of Marketing, helping to make a business seven figures per year. And she could have stayed, she could have settled.

But Laurie wanted the freedom to control how much she could make, when she could work and how she got to live her life. In 2019 Laurie left the corporate world behind her to start up her own business.

With £700 in her bank account.

After just six months of launching her business, she nearly gave up due to burnout from endless sales calls and live launching.

So, in 2019 I made it non-negotiable to launch my business and follow through, no matter what it took. Here I am!

Then, in 2020, Laurie found out she was unexpectedly pregnant. Putting an end to her 1:1s and sales calls, she turned her expertise into a course. She hit six figures that year.

As well as being a new mum, Laurie had recently lost both her dad and her nan - the two closest people to her in the world. Despite all the heartbreak and sleepless nights, she has gone from working in her bedroom and hiring her first employee in February 2021, to now having business that has generated millions in revenue.

If I'd given up again I wouldn't be where I am today. I wouldn't be celebrating hitting these six figure cash months. At the same time, it's clear that in that eight-year cycle of starting businesses and giving up I learned so much about what does and doesn't work in marketing. Eight years of learning, trial and error led to this business and success.

I have now helped thousands of people to do the same, to grow sustainable and scalable businesses that bring in consistent cash flow and passive income, all through turning their expertise into courses. And that's what I will teach you in this book. Let's begin!

The same is possible for you.

Laurie's website is www.laurieburrows.com

CELEBRITY GUEST
JAQUE ALMEIDA

My unstoppable story started when I was inside of my mum's belly. When I was born, the umbilical cord was around my neck and the doctor had to save my life. Growing up, my father was an alcoholic and left my mum when I was three years old. I was just a little girl, but I remember him beating my mum. My mother and my grandmother raised me until my mum found another guy. I was jealous of the time Mum spent with him and he was constantly comparing me to his own daughter. I didn't have the skills or knowledge to understand that I was feeling rejected; there was a lot of trauma. By the time I was fifteen years old, there was constant fighting between me, my mother and my step-father.

I clearly remember my fifteenth birthday when he bought a ticket for them both to go to a concert. I was left behind with my nanny. My grandmother was very special to me because she was always on my side, even though I was often judging my mum. These days, I understand how mum was torn between us, but at the time, it was hard. I was about 19 years old when I left home due to the conflicts between us all. I decided I needed to do something else and *live my life*.

At university, I worked two jobs to ensure I never stepped back. I was always moving forward because I felt I wanted more in life, not just a job that allowed me to pay my bills. I wanted to find my purpose.

I had been introduced to Jiu Jitsu when I was 21 years old and fell in love with the martial art at my very first training session; I didn't realise it was so much more than self-defence. I really didn't expect Jiu Jitsu would change my life in the way it did. It made me feel empowered, and that I would be able to achieve *anything*. My confidence began to increase from that very moment.

In fact, Jiu Jitsu was a big part in helping me to move forward from a very toxic relationship.

Some years later, I was in a relationship with a guy, with narcissistic tendencies, who treated me very badly. He insisted he loved me, but didn't respect me, and was constantly cheating on me. When I look back, I realise I didn't value and respect myself in relationships and that was reflected in my relationship with him. I hadn't had any good male role models, and never felt valued in those relationships, so it wasn't really surprising he treated me that way. Indeed, I needed to have that realisation to move forward. At the time, I also wasn't valued financially in my job. After three car accidents, (yes, three!) my attention was finally directed to the fact that I wasn't valuing myself. Leaving that relationship behind involved a lot of therapy, and along with my love of Jiu Jitsu, I was supported to finally move forward and value myself. I knew something needed to change.

Talking to my therapist, I discovered I had a deep belief that I should find a man, get married and have children, as that was all my mother had wanted for me. But I wanted more for my life. I had a friend who had spent some time in New Zealand, and when she came back, she was a different person. It took some soul-searching but I realised I didn't want to settle. Imagining myself in an apartment with a family felt like a great big 'no'. I was ready to fall in love with a new chapter of my life. I got a payout from one of the car accidents, and used it to move to Ireland in 2016.

Moving to a different country was the best thing I've ever done.

Although I am a passionate Brazilian and love my country, I didn't feel connected to my culture. I've always loved connecting with different people, with different thoughts, and sometimes I felt I just didn't fit in, although at the time it seemed crazy. However, when I first arrived in Ireland, I didn't speak any English. I got a job in a restaurant where my boss seemed to enjoy humiliating me. One time, he came home with me, offering me an 'extra job'. Just because I was Brazilian, and alone, he thought he could take advantage of me. I was devastated at how this new chapter of my life was going; I was homesick for my family and friends who could support me.

I decided I would stay in Ireland for six months, and after that, I would return home. That decision allowed me to embrace the situation, and I found a job in a hotel, as well as studying too. Although I was alone, as my travel buddy had already returned to Brazil, I suddenly felt like I was moving forward. When I started working at Subway, I met a great Irish guy, who patiently supported me to improve my English, and everything was going well. He was a fighter too and invited me to his gym to do some martial arts.

I finally started to meet new people and was introduced to the Irish culture … and I loved it. I became totally immersed in it, beginning to feel at home. It soon came to a point when I had to decide what to do next. I could only stay in Ireland for two years and my time was almost up. I had to either find a job with critical skills that would get me the visa I required, or go to university. I applied for many universities in Ireland, but my level of written English needed to much higher than I possessed, and so, I was not successful. There seemed to be so many barriers in my way. I did have a few people who suggested marriage to an Irish citizen as an option, but in my heart, I knew that wasn't the way forward. I wanted to do it by myself, on my own merits.

For the first time while living in Ireland, I decided to apply for jobs that needed the skills I was qualified in. I sent ten resume's every day, and I had faith that the 'right' job would come along. My visa was due to run out on 25th January, and on the 22nd, I had an interview where the guy offered me the position I needed to comply with my visa requirements, including sponsorship. I remember feeling overwhelmed and saying to myself, *my God … so you do exist.*

This was my first great achievement, and I can look back on that moment with pride. I was able to stay, on my own merits … I'd done it by myself. I hadn't had to compromise myself in any way. I stayed in that role for many years.

Throughout this time, I still had my Jiu Jitsu. If it wasn't for Jiu Jitsu, I don't think I would have made it in Ireland, Jui Jitsu instils courage, discipline, risk-taking, consistency and resilience; everything that shows up on the mat can be transcribed to my life. And in 2018, I began coaching where I had been training. I would coach ladies only. One day, a lady came to me and said, "Jackie, I'm only here because of you." I wondered why - questioning myself and my skills. "I'm going to send you a video…." she said. She sent me a recording of something that had been aired on TV; it was the story of how she was abused as a child, and later, how her husband had tried to kill her.

It was then I realised I was doing something different. It wasn't just a Jiu Jitsu class. I was empowering women and girls, often with a lot of trauma, helping them to feel confident and stay positive in their lives. I had discovered my purpose.

In 2022, I took another courageous leap; I decided to leave my job and just *go for it* - to work solely on my purpose of empowering women with trauma. A lot of things started to happen that year; I was moving forward at a rapid pace. One of those things, was that I did a TEDx talk. In preparation, I wrote down my story, and saw how my life has had its ups and downs. There were plenty of tears, but that's life. I recognised mine wasn't a simple story. I had been through a lot, but I valued everything that had happed to me. There were reasons for everything that happened, and I'd learned from every experience.

When I did the TEDx talk, it was a big milestone in my life, something I'd never imagined. It also opened a lot of doors for me. My TEDx talk was about how Jiu Jitsu had given me so much courage. It was then I decided I wanted to compete in the world championships. I didn't even have a coach, I just decided I was going.

Though when I arrived, I really started questioning myself on what I was even doing there. It was my best friend, Juan who reminded me of what I'd already achieved. He related the Bible story of David and how he'd gone to war with a small stone because he had a strategy to kill the giant …. and he did it. Slowly I began to believe in myself. I started to train really hard and acknowledge all that I'd done. I was fighting at the World Championships and I felt calm and happy. One day, I met a Brazilian coach who'd been working in Norway, and he said, "Jackie … you have the aura of champion. I can coach you … if you want."

He stayed to coach me through every single fight, and he believed in me. "You're the champ," he would say. "You can do it." To me, he was like an angel, knowing I was capable of it, allowing me to believe it myself.

I could hardly believe it when I found myself on the podium …. in first place. It felt like God's voice came to me in that moment, saying *you don't deserve anything less than the best.*

Everything was going well but I realised, despite me following my passion, I needed to be employed to get the long-term residency visa I required to stay in Ireland. So, I got myself a job for a period, but it was a lot of pressure on me, and there were many unrealistic goals to be met.

I didn't expect it at all, but in August, I experienced chronic burnout. I collapsed into a heap; I didn't even know my name or my age. I remember Juan shaking me, asking me my name, but I just couldn't remember. I was so burnt out, my friends had to call an ambulance. I felt like I was fighting to stay alive. It was the Jiu Jitsu that brought me back – because I am a fighter. I also had to connect with my spirituality and trust in my faith to keep going.

I left my high-pressured job, trying to do things on my own, but nothing was working out. But I kept praying and believing … and just kept going. This last year was a big one. I cried the whole year, regularly calling my mum on the other side of the world, just crying down the phone. Suddenly, I had a feeling of urgency … I had to return to Brazil. But I had no job and no money. Somehow, I managed to get there, and that's how I connected to the old Jackie.

Before I was home with my mum, who lives in a lovely place, I had visions of us praying together. When we did, we both cried. Soon after, I was able to move forward with forgiveness, talking to my step-father and my ex-boyfriend. I was actually forgiving myself. Letting go of the trauma, indeed, giving it back to them; it wasn't my trauma anymore.

A good friend of mine, was literally renting a house, over the middle of a waterfall. I went to stay with him, enjoying the wonderful nature of the place. The following day, I jumped into the waterfall, and it felt like I had cleansed my soul, like all the dirt had been removed and was floating on top of the water. It was so beautiful … I was, in essence, a new Jackie. That day, I felt like I was in a big globe, at the centre of everything. I finally understood why I'd experienced so much trauma … I didn't value myself enough; I didn't stand up for myself. I understood I could now pass on all I'd learned, so others don't have to make the mistakes I've made.

Another sign of moving forward, was that my coach presented me with my black belt in Jiu Jitsu. This signified to me that I was leaving the old Jackie behind, and I've overcome my problems. A black belt is more than just skills, more than just training. It's about community, having empathy for others and helping others. *I can now show the Jiu Jitsu.*

I can now teach everything God wants me to teach. I can teach women to be confident, and what to do when self-doubt creeps in; how to talk to themselves in an empowering way. Finally, I have found my purpose, and I'm super excited for the next chapter in life.

JAQUE ALMEIDA

J aque's life journey is one of resilience, transformation, and self-discovery. Born into a tumultuous environment marked by her father's absence, Jaque faced adversity from a young age. Despite the challenges she encountered, including a toxic relationship and professional setbacks, Jaque never lost sight of her desire for personal growth and fulfilment.

Her introduction to Jiu Jitsu became a turning point, instilling in her a sense of empowerment and purpose. Through the discipline of martial arts, Jaq found the strength to break free from destructive patterns and toxic relationships, ultimately realising her capacity for resilience and self-worth.

Moving to Ireland presented both opportunities and obstacles, yet Jaque embracing new experiences and immersing herself in the local culture. Despite initial difficulties, she found solace in her passion for Jiu Jitsu and began coaching others, recognising her ability to empower women and guide how overcoming their traumas.

Jaq's journey reached new heights when she decided to pursue her purpose wholeheartedly, leaving her job to focus on empowering women.

A TEDx talk and a remarkable victory at the World Championships, her resilience and determination, affirming her belief in herself and her abilities.

However, Jaq's path was not without its challenges. Burnout and personal struggles tested her, leading her on a journey of spiritual and emotional healing. Returning to Brazil proved to be a transformative experience, allowing her to reconnect with her own essence and confront past traumas with forgiveness and acceptance.

Receiving her black belt in Jiu Jitsu symbolised more than just skill, it signified Jaq's evolution into a beacon of strength and guidance for others.

As Jaq embarks on the next chapter of her life, she does so with gratitude, excitement, and a deep sense of fulfilment, knowing that she has found her true calling and is ready to make a positive impact on the world.

Jaque's website is www.jaquelinealmeida.com

I AM SHE. SHE IS ME.
I AM FINALLY FREE!
LELJLA DAUTI

From the outside looking, to most people it would look like I had it all. I grew up with both my parents, and it would have looked like my siblings and myself never wanted or needed anything. That theme carried through into my adult life. But what people didn't realise was that there was a dirty secret I've been hiding all these years – I've been a victim of domestic abuse from my early childhood. My dad was the first perpetrator. And then into my adulthood, my husband (now ex-husband) was an abuser too. I grew up in Kosovo, and from the moment I was born, all I knew was violence. At the time, we were living under Serbia's genocidal regime, and we were victims of ethnic cleansing and genocide. My family were publicly resisting the regime at the time, and we fled to the UK as asylum seekers.

Pretty much from the moment I was born, violence and abuse was part of my life; I didn't know anything different. When I reached the age of twenty-nine, things didn't feel right anymore. It was almost as if a veil was lifted. I began questioning everything and started going to therapy. I first went to see a counsellor because I thought I was going crazy. I thought there must be something wrong with me. Thankfully, with the help of my therapist, I came to realise there was nothing wrong with me at all, but what I'd been subjected to, by everyone else around me … was wrong. I realised I was a victim of domestic abuse and violence throughout my life.

I'd been living with my husband for eight-and-a-half years at that point and realised I had to come up with a way to flee that environment too. I'd gone from fleeing my home country to growing up with my dad being a perpetrator, and then suddenly finding myself living with another perpetrator. I'd done nothing about it, as it was what I had experienced throughout my entire life.

I ended up escaping that relationship, with my daughter, in October 2019. We all know what happened in March 2020, with the whole world going into lockdown. The world as we knew it, ended, and a new world, a new life, began. We all had to stop.

I was working from home and fresh from leaving a super traumatic period of my life. I wondered what I would do with all of the trauma I'd experienced … how would I process it? I didn't even know where to begin. I discovered that after the crisis level of abuse has ended, being that I had left and was physically safe, there was very little support I could receive after that. There seemed to be no support for *the survivor*. No matter where I searched, literally trolling all over the Internet, I couldn't find any forums, communities or support networks.

By this time, I was desperate, and very depressed during lockdown. I didn't know what to do or where to turn. But I knew something had to give, something had to change, because I could not carry the pain. I just couldn't process anything. I felt like in my whole life as I knew it, had ended. I had no outlet, no way to express how I felt, no way to recover from what I'd experienced.

So, in October 2020, I had a revelation. *Sometimes, if you can't see the change, you've must be the change.* I decided to film a story from my own history on my old iPhone and called it: *My sister was killed by her boyfriend.* It was what it said on the tin. It was the story of someone who was very close to me.

The content we consume these days on social media is really fast paced. My video is seven minutes long and I truly believed that absolutely nobody would watch it. But I posted it anyway, and settled in to the comfort that, if it helped *just one woman*, I would be happy with that.

The story went viral … overnight. I went from 400 friends and family to over 20,000 female survivors of domestic abuse.

Within a week, the video had nearly 3 million views. To me, it was indicative of how much the space was needed, how desperate women were. Female survivors needed somewhere safe to be seen and heard. After that video, I was getting thousands of messages and emails from women asking me to share their stories. That was the birth of **Layla**. I began by sharing survival stories on behalf of other female survivors of domestic abuse. They were real life stories, and women trusted me and my platform to anonymously share their stories on their behalf. They were told in first person, and they were real stories. Since then, I haven't stopped, and it's continued to evolve. It was only about nine months before women began coming forward publicly and saying, *I don't want to be anonymous anymore. I don't want to be faceless. I want to be seen, I want to be heard and I want the world to see me for the pain I've been through.*

I was asked to be part of a documentary on a major broadcasting channel, but unfortunately two days before filming, the producers got back to me and said; "We've had a chat with our legal team, and you can't be a part of the show because you don't have a conviction against your perpetrator." That hit me hard. I couldn't believe it, as the thought of going for a conviction had never even occurred to me. I'd been subjected to pain and abuse for so long, nearly a decade, and now I'd been invalidated. I didn't realise there could be a barrier to getting my story out there.

As a creator and entrepreneur at heart, I knew I could get the message out there myself and amplify the voices of survivors. I decided not to put control in the hands of others. So, in June 2021, I created a documentary series called *The Survivors*, off the back of women wanting to break their silence and come forward publicly, along with women doing things when we feel we've been hugely wronged or there is a massive sense of injustice.

We've filmed four seasons, giving women the voice and the space to feel seen and heard - so, they don't have judgement, they don't have shame, they don't have blame. We know as survivors, that too often when we come forward, even at the first point of call of reporting it to services like the police or anyone that's supposed to help us, we're immediately met with questions like, *why didn't you just leave? Why **didn't** you fight back? Why **did** you fight back?*

These types of questions lead the victims to feel like they are being *blamed,* instead of questioning *why did the abuser choose to abuse?* Because we know there is no other cause for abuse, other than choice. It's really as simple as that.

I wanted to create a safe space for women where they could come forward and share their stories, and this lit a thirst and a fire in me. Sharing these stories is important and holding a space for these women is fantastic. It's made me feel fulfilled in my own life and has helped on my own recovery journey. Though it still didn't feel like it was enough. I knew that systemically and structurally, things still needed to change. I turned the docu-series into a domestic abuse awareness campaign. Since then, laws and bills have been passed as a direct result of the women in my community coming forward and sharing their stories. In fact, Erica Sackway, an amazing woman who took part in my first season, ended up changing the statute of limitations of reporting common assault in England and Wales from six months to 24 months, because there's no constitution for domestic abuse being a crime in England and Wales.

As victims and survivors, if our abusers are convicted, most of the prosecutions are labelled as common assault, GBH, ABH, depending on what the crime was. It's prosecuted as if a stranger committed the crime (unless it's prosecuted under coercive control, which only came into effect recently). It's still quite difficult to get convictions under that. But it's the ripples, that turn into waves and then into tsunamis that start creating incredible change, not just societally, but systemically, too. I've seen famous people coming forward, sharing their stories and bringing a light to domestic abuse. We know that abuse is not just violence; it's not just the violence that makes it abusive. This is a significant message I want to get across, along with changing the language we use when we talk about domestic abuse, when we engage with survivors, when we engage with victims. This is really important. I've shaped the campaign to a point where it's gone from not just changing lives, but to saving lives. It's now made people sit up and think, "wow, something must be done here."

Ultimately, we must continue to ask how we can help change these women's lives. We must continue to work on giving women the tools they need to recover.

LELJLA DAUTI

Lejla Dauti is the founder and director of Lejla Please Tell My Story, a non-profit organisation and online community dedicated to raising awareness about domestic abuse for female survivors. As a survivor herself, Lejla creates documentaries that share survival stories of her community with a trailblazing goal to influence systemic changes.

Lejla is on a mission to provide safe spaces for women to share their stories and remind them they are not alone. Lejla is a fierce feminist who advocates for women's rights and supports female victims of domestic abuse, whilst creating a culture of awareness, intervention and prevention.

Lejla leads with empathy and compassion in her work and aims to create change that directly benefits women in her community and beyond. She is passionate about using her skills and resources to make a positive impact in the lives of women who have experienced abuse and is dedicated to helping them move from survival to thriving.

Lelja's website is www.lptms.co.uk

IN HONOUR OF NATALIA
MAGDELENA McMORROW

Turning 40 this year, I'm a mature student at the university of Silgo, currently in my second and final year of a master's degree in social work, finishing in May and graduating in November. In June, I'll be starting on a graduate programme with our child protection services here in Ireland.

Born in Poland and living there until I was twenty-two years old, I got my bachelor's degree in pedagogy in Poland before, deciding to move to Ireland. I was engaged at the time and came to Ireland just to try to make a bit of money to get married. But then I fell in love with Ireland and split with my fiancé because I saw an opportunity to live a little first.

I called off the wedding, stayed in Ireland, and worked a variety of different jobs, in clothes shops, in a call centre, a pub and a restaurant, before deciding to open up my own business doing nails, which I was trained in. By 2012, I'd married an Irishman, and we had a little boy.

Living in a small town, I quickly became one of the go-to nail technicians and for five years I was doing quite well. I got talking with one of my clients who worked for residential services in Sligo. She said that with my degree, I could change my line of work, as they were always looking for staff. I realised I didn't have a great head for business, but I was a good people person, that's why my business was doing well. But

I'd had enough of being self-employed, so thought I'd give residential services a go.

I started working in residential care and loved the job, though it was often very demanding. I was a social care worker, supporting children in care living in residential homes. Our shifts were round the clock, with the kids needing 24-hour care.

In the meantime, my sister moved to live in Ireland with her husband and two children. I was happy to have her closeby, our two brothers were still in Poland. When my sister was turning 30, after they'd had another boy, she decided to split from her husband. He didn't want them to split up, but she was adamant. One day, I was finishing a 24-hour shift, when he told me she didn't make it home after a night out. I became very anxious because it wasn't like her to go out partying. She would never leave the kids or just disappear.

I rang all my friends, and people she was out with, and nobody had heard from her. I decided straightaway to call the Garda. They took it very seriously from the minute I rang them, and they told me to bring a picture. The search started on 29 April 2018 and her husband was arrested that evening. I didn't think he would have anything to do with it, but it turned out that he did.

He had strangled her in the morning when she'd come home and hidden her body in the forest, before he told me she'd gone missing. He was held for two days, and the Garda had a fair idea going by the CCTV that he'd done it, but they had to let him go because they didn't have the proof. But then he rang me. I went out to meet him and he told me he knew where her body was, and that he'd found her dead in the house, so he hid the body.

I actually backed him up because I didn't think he was capable of hurting her. But suddenly, an idea started to fester that maybe he did have something to do with it. When the body was found, he was arrested again, and he eventually admitted to me that he had killed her, though he wouldn't talk to the Garda. I still couldn't believe he was capable of it; he'd been my brother-in-law for twelve years. I suppose I didn't want to believe it.

I supported him through the first few weeks in prison, but then things started adding up and I began catching him on his lies. When I told him I wouldn't be visiting him anymore, he lost it with me as well. Two years later, he was convicted of murder and sentenced to life in prison, though in Ireland that means he probably will be out in the next ten years. So, the three children were left and we didn't know what we were going to do.

The law in Ireland is slightly different, and I convinced my brother to move here and take care of the boys, as he didn't have children of his own, and I thought it would be better if they stayed. So, I managed to secure a rental for him and the kids, and got in touch with welfare and to get payments for him so he could look after the children.

During this time, I was promoted in my job to a deputy manager of one of the residential homes, but I suppose I was mentally struggling. I ended up separating from my husband and quitting my job as I'd hit rock bottom. I went into party mode, not having the kids on the weekend, and honestly, I fell apart. It took me about a year to get myself together again.

And then Covid hit and I decided I needed to do something for myself again. I actually went back to doing nails. I worked in a salon as well as having my own small nail bar. But I still was searching for what I wanted to do and I ended up deciding to get my master's degree in social work. I quit the nails and went into full time study. In 2022, I was a single mum of two, studying for my master's degree.

In the meantime, I became interested in finding out more about domestic abuse and in my placement, I went into community mental health. My practise teacher in my placement, Mariet, had a high interest in domestic abuse, and together we went to a conference in Enniskillen, organised by Women's Aid.

At that conference, there was a speaker called Jane Moncton Smith, from the UK and I've now watched her in different documentaries around domestic abuse and homicide. She was taking questions and I managed to speak to her about my sister and how we didn't see any signs of domestic abuse. She explained how difficult it can be to spot them.

Unless you start researching and learning about it, the signs are very difficult to see, but now I know the signs. I realise that when he was threatening to kill himself, the thought of killing was in his head already, and it turned on my sister.

I don't want my sister to be forgotten. I want people to be aware of the signs of domestic abuse, and how it can end up as homicide. I don't think people are aware of how easily domestic abuse can escalate. I remember my sister saying that she didn't feel threatened, but I would regularly suggest she should move out.

She would always say. "why would I move out? I have three kids." I guess it made sense at the time, but even if I saw the signs, could I have saved her? I don't know.

I like to think that things happen for a reason. Maybe if all that didn't happen, I wouldn't be where I am today, helping others. That's how I want to see it. Last year was five years since my sister was murdered, so I organised a fundraiser in Sligo for our local domestic abuse charity.

They staff are government funded but they still need a lot of support, and all the money goes to the women who need it. It was literally a month before the anniversary, and last minute I knew I needed to organise something.

My sister loved fitness, so I contacted our local fitness studio and asked them to help. They were sceptical as it was such last minute, but they went for it. We booked the astro pitch in town and put it out on Facebook, Instagram and everywhere we could.

I actually have goosebumps thinking about it because it was just such a brilliant day. We had a Metafit class and Kango jump, and then the local doggy daycare joined us as well for a dog walk. We sold raffle tickets and I didn't even have to reach out to local businesses, because they were reaching out to me, offering me prizes for the raffle. We ended up raising about three and a half thousand euro within a couple of hours.

I was blown away by the turnout and the amount of money we've raised. It was just such a positive day.

I never realised how on edge I would be and how it affected me, as the date gew closer to the anniversary day as it came around every year. It's her birthday as well, on 12th April, so the whole month of April is difficult for me. But last year was the first time I actually turned the day into something positive.

The local domestic violence agency asked if I'd like to be on their board of management, which I said yes to. Though of course, finishing my master's in my priority in my busy life, along with taking care of my children. Of course, I regularly see my nephews for sleepovers too, as they live in the same town.

I don't know what my future holds, but I know I will continue to work in Social Care and Child Protection. I also know that I will continue to bring attention to domestic violence. It's something we must all be aware of.

MAGDELENA MCMORROW

Hello, I'm Magdalena Mc Morrow, a mature MA student in Social Work and a proud single mother of two wonderful children. My academic journey is infused with a rich tapestry of life experiences that shape my perspective on social work.

My deep commitment to advocacy and raising awareness about domestic abuse is fueled by a personal connection to the devastating impact of this issue. Tragically, my sister became a victim of domestic homicide, igniting a fervent desire within me to make a difference.

In my academic pursuits, I aim to integrate my personal insights with theoretical and practical knowledge gained through my studies. I aspire to contribute meaningfully to the field, addressing the complex challenges associated with domestic abuse.

Beyond academia, I actively engage with community initiatives, support networks, and awareness campaigns related to domestic abuse. My goal is to use my lived experiences to bring attention to the realities of domestic violence, fostering empathy and advocating for the rights and safety of survivors.

As I continue my academic journey, I remain committed to making a positive impact on the lives of those affected by domestic abuse. My story reflects resilience, empathy, and the transformative power of personal experiences in driving meaningful change.

THE GATEWAY TO MY
LITTLE GIRL
GERALDINE McGRATH

*I*n the depths of adulthood, with all the responsibilities of life, there exists *the most beautiful treasure within; the inner child. It's the spark of spirited curiosity and endless wonder that never truly fades. This chapter is your gateway to begin to rediscover and nurture your inner child, your source of playfulness, joy, creativity, and the resilience waiting to be rekindled within you.*

At the young age of 2 years 4 months, recovering from measles and following a prolonged febrile convulsion, I faced the harrowing ordeal of an anaphylactic reaction, triggered by penicillin. This remarkable incident, occurring in only 0.02% to 0.04% of the population, left an indelible mark on my life.

For 48 hours, the life of 'Geraldine McGrath' became very uncertain; she was in a critical condition.

After a gruelling 48 hours, my condition gradually began to improve, but I was required to remain hospitalised for an additional three weeks; a young girl of only two years old, wrenched away from her family.

In my Mums words:

"The ambulance crew just grabbed you and put you on the machines, with the lights going and the noise of the sirens, it seemed like I was living a nightmare. When we got to the hospital, they let me see you for just two minutes, then the nurse was told to 'get Mum out.' It was your Dad's first day in a new job, and thankfully, it was just down the road from the hospital. The Doctor come out to tell us you were allergic to penicillin. He said, 'we can only do what we can, but we have a very poorly little girl in there.' We were the luckiest parents to get you back to normal after three weeks in hospital, but what followed, was many visits to Manchester University Hospital, alongside many sessions of speech therapy. Travelling on the bus to speech therapy, I had to keep telling you to put your tongue in - I would be mortified as you did it so many times, but we would ended up laughing together, my sweet brave little girl."

Childhood illness can result in an inner child disconnection. Given the need to navigate complex emotions and challenges related to the illness, it can fast-track maturity, creating a gap between the child and their inner playful self. These experiences may overshadow the child's natural curiosity and playfulness, and initiate the arrival of persistent feelings of isolation, anxiety and fear. Healing involves addressing these past traumas to rediscover a sense of freedom and joy.

This may impact the development of self-identity. To initiate healing, individuals must confront these past traumas and re-establish their connection with their capacity for freedom, playfulness and joy.

The trauma I had faced at such a tender age, was a shadow that would re-emerge sporadically, casting its cloud over various moments and phases of my life.

From as young as I can remember, loving, curious, happy and carefree is how I would describe myself as a little girl. I had a huge love for people and treasured the beautiful connections and friendships I had with children and adults. One of my most important realisations, was the beautiful diversity I was surrounded by.

One of many happy spaces at my primary school was the outdoor playground, where a bench was positioned close by the gate beneath the beautiful trees.

As one of five girls, I've been blessed with my sisters; Rosie, Dean, Shelly and Sinead. I was the middle child, living in a very busy home, growing up with my 4 sisters. I recall their love for their toys, though I struggled to enjoy toys. My happiness was discovered in moments of curiosity. These moments were usually found amongst overhearing adult conversations. My curiosity come alive, puzzling together in my child's mind my own perception and meaning of life.

I always put my heart deeply into everything and give my very best. I can still recall bringing Mum out of a place of stress, encouraging her to hear the echoes of laughter throughout the house.

I recall rising in the early hours of the morning, to put my legs between the stair banisters and watch my Dad leave for work. Yet from a young age, I felt a sense of maturity, manoeuvring the shopping trolley down Tesco's aisles, as my mother attended to my younger sister. When Mum arrived, I would be ecstatic to share the bargains I had discovered along the way. I was often described as a young person with the soul of someone who has lived before.

A treasury of delightful memories was crafted within the walls of our family home, the embrace of the garden, the halls of school, in the company of friends, during family festivities, through Brownies and Irish dances, on joyful outings to the park, during holidays, and more. Reflecting on over a decade of cherished childhood moments fills my heart with immense love and gratitude.

However, alongside the treasury, I experienced a profound detachment from my inner child. This manifested in an unusual reliance on adult company, a disinterest in typical childhood delight and an accelerated maturity. This was accompanied by a persistent sense of fear and anxiety I couldn't quite understand.

In April 1992, our family would move from Manchester to Ireland.

My parents were both born in Ireland and we relocated to where my dad grew up. Our newly built home awaited us. So much love, hard work and sacrifice went into making this dream happen.

A child carrying the wounds of their inner child may often struggle to handle change, like moving to a new place, because of the emotional scars from previous experiences. Such situations can trigger emotions of anxiety, fear and resistance in times of transition.

It becomes vital to offer emotional support and guidance to assist the child in navigating and adjusting to these changes, while also tending to the emotional needs of their inner child.

I only had two months left of primary school to complete in Ireland. The loving, happy, curious, and carefree girl was ready to start her new chapter. I honestly can't recall a lot from this short time. I connected quickly with some lovely girls, however, I remember going from a feeling of acceptance to rejection, during this time.

Within two months, a young girl learned an unkind lesson about the world's perception of beauty. It was a far cry from what she believed about herself, as she faced teasing for her short haircut, her body shape and her distinct Mancunium accent. My life transformed significantly during that time. Despite the promise of a summer filled with family time, the looming thought of starting high school cast a shadow of dread. The only comfort was knowing I would be joined there by my two older sisters.

My high school experience was marked by tough times, as I often felt anxious when walking down the corridors, with the echoes of songs chanted to me. Bullying was a presence in my life from the first year to the third year, and I genuinely felt lost and overwhelmed. Most days, after school, I sought refuge in sleep, hoping I wouldn't have to face those painful feelings again the next day. On the worse days, I prayed I wouldn't have to wake up again.

However, even in those dark moments, there was a glimmer of hope.

Every weekend, I accompanied my Mum to the markets, where we worked together to set up our stall; it always looked so beautiful. In this environment, I found a place where I was not judged, and even my accent was embraced and accepted. I made meaningful connections at the markets.

In school, I also created strong bonds with many girls in my year, as well as a few boys. It was during my final two years that I slowly gained a sense of confidence and began to find moments of enjoyment in life.

In September 1997, after a lot of persuasion with my parents, I moved to Wigan with my big sister, Rosie. The deal was struck when we agreed we would stay with my cousin. The day arrived. It was time to hug Mum and Dad goodbye and as the van drove away, I felt my heart jump out of my body. For the first time in my life, I wouldn't be relying on my mum and dad.

I went on to spend almost eight months in Wigan with Rosie … and loved it so much - once I settled. I found much more than education would ever bring me; I found a connection to myself. I also found karaoke and Whitney Houston – I found *The Greatest Love of All* and would belt it out at karaoke on a Sunday evening.

Returning to Ireland, I had become almost unrecognisable to those who knew me. One particular night stands out. While out with my friend at Nero's in Donegal. Catching my reflection in a long mirror after leaving the ladies, the glitter of my miniskirt and belly top seemed to echo the inner shine I was feeling in that moment.

A period of fun times followed, filled with lively weekends, working in hospitality. Then, on a memorable evening in July 1998, my friend-convinced me to venture out to Pettigo. It was there that I crossed paths with Declan, who would become my husband. And that encounter marked the beginning of our shared story.

We have been blessed beyond words with our four beautiful children, Craig (23), Kristen (18), Courtney (15) & Kiana (8). In May 2024, we will be celebrating twenty years of marriage. It's been quite the trip – full of good times, exciting adventures, new chapters, as well as some tough challenges along the way, but through it all, there's been a whole lot of love.

THE JOURNEY TO MY LITTLE GIRL

In 2015, we were blessed with the birth of our daughter Kiana. Maternity leave brought a slower pace and heightened self-awareness, allowing me to cherish our childrens' summer holidays and recognise the precious moments I'd previously missed. This period was an emotional reminder of how quickly our children grow and the importance of cherishing these times. It was a truly transformative time in my life.

The changes continued to evolve and arrive. In 2016, I had the opportunity to join Network Marketing. I recall my first conference in Dublin; I hadn't experienced inspiration and motivation on this level, ever before. Looking to the stage for a split second I had a thought - *Maybe one day I will be up there as a speaker.* Instantly, my inner critic shut me down; *you will never be good enough for that.*

Late in 2016 I had a surprise pregnancy, though sadly at twelve weeks pregnant, I experienced my first miscarriage. As one of the most difficult journeys I've ever had to experience, the sense of loss felt all too much for me to cope with. I sat in a very dark space throughout this time, however, this would shape my path ahead.

I faced a significant decision in 2017, one that marked a turning point after dedicating twelve years of my life to the family business that had shaped my twenties and early thirties. I made the tough choice to resign, which lead to a challenging and solitary period in my life. However, this decision opened doors to numerous opportunities. My journey continued with Network Marketing, where I achieved a remarkable milestone in December 2020, placing me in the top 1% of the company worldwide. Interestingly though, I soon discovered that achieving such success externally, didn't provide the inner fulfilment I had been seeking.

From that point on, new possibilities unwrapped, as I immersed myself into self-improvement and personal growth. I delved into mind-set work, meditation

and gratitude, beginning a journey of deep self-discovery. Along the way, I experimented with many holistic approaches and engaged in numerous healing modalities, including counselling, coaching, Rapid Transformational Therapy (RTT).

THE LOCKED GATE

I found that I was deeply passionate about these transformative practices and began to identify that the gateway to my little girl had been firmly locked, all the way through my childhood and well into my adulthood.

In 2018, following many therapy sessions, it was very clear that I had been using perfectionism as a coping strategy throughout my life. My life had been shadowed by self-doubt, overthinking and procrastination. Pleasing others was second nature to me, yet I retained a sense of honesty that was also aimed at bringing joy to others. Importantly, the concept of personal boundaries was foreign to me; I hadn't understood the role strong boundaries played in life.

Perfectionism can lead to a disconnection from one's inner child by creating a relentless pursuit of flawlessness, often rooted in childhood experiences. This pursuit can overshadow the inner child's need for play, creativity, and making mistakes.

UNSEEN SCARS: THE INNER CHILD'S IMPACT ON ADULT LIFE

Many thoughts and feelings can be experienced by your wounded inner child:

- *Persistent Sadness or Depression* - A persistent feeling of unhappiness or hollowness that might not be linked to current life events.

- *Anxiety and Fear* - Worries, often about future abandonment or disloyalty, and a general sense of insecurity.
- *Anger* - Unexplained anger or irritation, which can be a defence mechanism to hide more vulnerable feelings.
- *Shame* - A deep rooted belief that one is intrinsically flawed or unworthy of love and happiness.
- *Distrust* - A scepticism of others' intentions, making it hard to form close relationships.
- *Loneliness* - Even when surrounded by others, there might be a sense of isolation or disconnection.
- *Inadequacy* - Relentless thoughts that one is not good enough, smart enough, or gifted enough.
- *Guilt* - Recurrent guilt over past actions, feeling responsible for things beyond one's control.
- *Indecisiveness* - Difficulty making decisions due to fear of making the wrong choice.
- *Perfectionism* - An internal pressure to be perfect, often to earn approval or love.
- *Self-Sabotage* - Engaging in behaviours that challenge personal success or happiness.
- *Regret* - An obsession with the past and what might have been.

These feelings and thoughts often stem from unresolved childhood emotions and can significantly impact an adult's daily life and relationships. Healing the inner child involves acknowledging these feelings, understanding their origins, and often, seeking therapeutic support to work through them.

Reconnecting with the inner child involves addressing these perfectionist tendencies, learning to embrace imperfection, and cultivating self-compassion. It's about reconnecting with the part of oneself that finds joy in the journey, not just the destination.

The lock of the gateway to my little girl loosened after I completed my TEDx talk in August 2021. Do you have the courage to be Imperfectly

Perfect?

This was the first time I shared my inner trauma. This soon to become a turning point in my life.

I identified a huge disconnection with my inner child, and maybe this had surfaced from my early trauma from my severe illness. It's also possible I've carried intergenerational trauma as there is deep trauma on both sides of my parents' families. This is trauma both my parents endured, as well as intergenerational trauma.

Intergenerational trauma is the passing down of emotional and psychological wounds from one generation to the next, often due to experiences of significant trauma, oppression or adversity in a family's history.

Following my TEDx, I become super curious to explore my inner child. I completed many teachings, each one representing a different piece of my puzzle. I experienced the knowing that I had a huge disconnection from my inner child. I felt I had left my little girl somewhere; the disconnection felt miles apart.

THE KEY TO UNLOCKING THE GATE

The next message showed up with a sense of urgency. I took mum with me to visit family and friends, when I took a trip to Manchester, in September 2022, to attend an event. We arrived in Manchester airport and took the train to Manchester Piccadilly. I remember getting a picture with Mum, and as I breathed in, I felt my little girl closer.

During our bus ride to Old Trafford, I expressed a desire to visit my primary school near our old home. Mum doubted access so late in the day, but I felt certain, already having envisioned it. Sure enough, in just ten minutes, we completed a tour of the school and proceeded to the playground, a place of fond memories where a younger, joyful and outgoing Geraldine played freely.

While mum and the caretaker chatted, I was drawn to a spot filled with recollections of laughter and friendship. A place where a bench once stood—a bench rich with conversations, farewell photos with friends, and next to a gate through which I once eagerly ran to school.

It happened. I created the most beautiful, powerful connection. I called my beautiful little girl back. My little girl had been kept safe in a place I knew and loved, but it was time, to lift her up, to hold her tight, to bring her back to Ireland where she belonged. We reconnected as one. It was my 42nd year and the gate had flung open, once again.

THE MAGIC DEEPENED

One winter's evening after our trip, as I listened to '80s music on MTV. I was captivated when Whitney Houston's *The Greatest Love of All* started playing. I'd loved the song but had never seen the video. A profound moment unfolded that would last a lifetime: witnessing Whitney's adult and child selves walk towards each other on stage, merging into one.

As I shared earlier, during my time in Wigan, not only did I find myself, I found karaoke, I found Whitney Houston, I found The Greatest Love of All.

Paulo Coelho once said ~ *When you want something, all the universe conspires in helping you to achieve it.*

The power of the message I received sparked a profound curiosity within me, leading me to pursue an *Inner Child Healing Diploma*. This allowed me to incorporate this transformative work into my practice, not only as a mentor and coach, but also as an Inner Child Therapist.

RECONNECTING WITH MY LITTLE GIRL

My little girl is a loving and curious, with an imaginative spirit, always eager to learn, explore and find joy in the simplest of things; always true and proud of being *Geraldine*. It's a reminder of the wonder and innocence that exists within me. Together we are a force of nature.

Reconnecting with my little girl opened my world. It's reignited my creative spark and facilitated deep emotional healing from past wounds. I now experience life more fully from a place of joy and freedom. It's deepened and enriched my personal relationships through greater empathy and open-heartedness. It has provided me with the clarity that my soul's purpose and fulfilment are waiting along my path.

This reconnection also served as a powerful solution to stress, encouraging me to engage with the world with my sense of curiosity and wonder. Embracing my inner child helped me to shed the constraints of perfectionism, allowing for a more compassionate and authentic life.

I embarked on a journey of self-awareness and self-acceptance, realising that healing is an ongoing process. I understood I wouldn't wake up one morning with all my pain gone; instead, it was a journey of growth and continuous improvement.

EMBRACING THE HEART'S ECHO

A Journey of Love and Spirituality in Reconnecting with Your Inner Child.

Connecting with your inner child is a personal and unique journey, which unfolds in its own time. It can be very painful and emotional, whereby professional and holistic therapies may play a key support for you.

Initiating the journey to connect with your inner child can begin by setting aside moments for reflection and revisiting pastimes you delighted in during your early years, whether it's music, playing a game, visiting a place you loved in your younger years or indulging in the simplicity of daydreams.

Mindfulness practices, such as meditation, can anchor you in the here and now, much like the immersive way children live. Writing to your younger self in a journal can be releasing, offering a chance for compassion and self-recognition.

Welcome all your emotions with open arms, treating yourself with the same kindness and acceptance a child would seek. By tuning in to and affirming your internal dialogue, you honour the purest part of your being.

This path to reconnection nurtures the essence of who you are, allowing you to re-engage with the natural sense of joy, curiosity, and awe every child knows.

Explore various therapies and holistic approaches to find what resonates with you personally. Your path to well-being is distinct, and the methods that will help you may be very different to the journey I've travelled.

This congruence leads to greater life satisfaction, purposeful living, emotional well-being, and the ability to maintain enlightening continuity. It simplifies life's choices and supports the creation of a meaningful legacy.

PLAYGROUND ROOTS TO ADULT REWARDS

THE GRATIFICATION OF ALIGNED VALUES

The most fascinating realisation was the alignment between the values of my younger years and those I hold as an adult. In 2021, when I began delving into what I truly value, it was evident that *Love, Curiosity* and *Integrity* stood at the core. Peeling back the layers of my early years, it's apparent how these values were present in my youthful excitement and in my genuine contentment with being Geraldine during my first decade of life.

In essence, a close alignment between childhood and adult values offers an unwavering foundation for decision-making and a strong sense of identity, which contributes to resilience and authentic relationships.

Whitney Houston's resonating lyrics, serve as a powerful reminder that true healing and self-love begin from within, starting with our inner child. It is this inner healing that carves the path to genuine self-appreciation. Self-love is an overarching feeling of acceptance and care for oneself, while active appreciation for oneself involves taking concrete actions which express and reinforce that love through self-care and personal growth.

Unlock the gateway to the power of reconnecting with your inner child, guided by the compass of love, curiosity, and integrity, and witness the transformative journey of your life – Geraldine McGrath

GERALDINE MCGRATH

Geraldine McGrath stands out as a celebrated voice with her award-winning podcast and her influential role as a speaker, mentor, educator, and leader. She's the passionate creator behind the "I Am Unstoppable" movement and warmly invites you to be part of a life-altering journey. By sharing her own shift from chasing the illusion of perfection to welcoming her authentically imperfect self, Geraldine highlights the raw fuel of self-awareness as the key to breaking away from restrictive patterns and behaviours. As an Inner Child Therapist, Geraldine inspires you to discover your greatest treasure within your inner child.

Her goal is to activate individuals to explore and embrace their inherent strengths and passions. Geraldine trusts that by cultivating a deep sense of self-awareness, everyone has the power to tap into their maximum potential, overcome barriers, and make a substantial difference in the world.

As the creator of "Radiate Realness," Geraldine forges a space for heartfelt and raw conversations, fostering empowerment through collective stories. Dedicated to suicide prevention, she leads weekly dialogues to dismantle stigmas and encourage openness.

Geraldine's gift for honest and passionate speech has also led her to become an inspiring figure on the speaking path, including delivering a TEDx talk titled "Do You Have the Courage to be Imperfectly Perfect," where she advocates for the beauty in our imperfections as avenues for growth.

Serving as the Communication Lead for TEDx Enniskillen in 2022 was a highlight for her, sharing in the growth of 22 TEDx speakers.

In her role as a mentor, coach, and trainer, she focuses on fostering natural leadership, guiding others through their personal journeys of discovery and empowerment.

With additional roles as a Suicide First Aid Tutor and an Addictions Trainer, Geraldine reaffirms her commitment to supporting those facing personal challenges and holds mental health close to her heart.

Through "I Am Unstoppable," and as a healer, she's on a mission to spark a global movement that encourages people to break free from their mental constraints and embrace authentic freedom. By fostering self-awareness and self-empowerment, she envisions a world where individuals can access their unlimited potential and drive positive change for themselves and for others.

Geraldine beckons you to join her from a place of feeling confined to a state of boundless possibility, urging you to celebrate your true self, your unstoppable self and shine your unique light, leaving a lasting positive mark on the world.

Igniting the spark of an idea for this book, bringing together kindred spirits as co-authors, and creating 'Unstoppable Stories' with 24 extraordinary women has been an exhilarating journey that soared beyond my own dreams. This collaboration has amplified a wave of inspiration, it will touch many lives and serve a purpose throughout the world that eclipses beyond our individual stories.

STRENGTH IN THE
FACE OF ADVERSITY
PAULA ESSON

My unstoppable story started when I was about five years old. I grew up in Brazil on an air base, as my father is a geologist, and he was working out there. My mum has an incredible memory of me going past her on a motorbike, at the age of four … without a helmet on. I was with a gorgeous looking young Brazilian, travelling at about 70 miles per hour. I remember that the tray of juice and biscuits she was carrying hit the floor and I spent a lot of time in my bedroom that afternoon … but that was the start of my unstoppable story. Having just turned 54, I can say that, in my entire lifetime, I've never been *bolted down*. It's not that I'm anti-society or anti-establishment or anything like that, indeed I'm very much a conformist, however, I just feel that the beauty and integrity of this world has to be explored, and that we can expand our thinking and our appreciation of what's achievable. It's a feeling that continues to rise up inside of me.

I don't know if anybody else recognises this feeling, but for me, it's almost like a level of excitement that can get out of control. It's like the roar of a lion or the shout of tribal master. Once you're absolutely, totally in alignment with yourself, you feel a rise of energy that comes up in the core and [almost] explodes out of your mouth. Though usually, when it happens, I'm sitting in some sort of boring meeting, where it's not always appropriate to freely express my feelings. I've had to work on this rebelliousness. Having said that, I wasn't a rebellious child; I was an unstoppable child, which meant I was a bit of a handful.

Being adopted, I was lucky to end up with the 'right' parents. I was a little bundle of energy, always on the move. Movement is my key and I would be into everything. under everything, up to everything; particularly in terms of climbing or sport. For example, I would undertake absolutely every adventure I could. It was my innate curiosity that drove my personality … and still does. This little cute, mini, unstoppable kid who was just full of abundance and energy, became a fun-magnet. People would say, "if you want to have some fun … go find Paula."

I always seemed to put myself in a position where I found myself with wonderful opportunities. My attitude was, *what have I got to lose?* I was always willing to give things a try. At 16, I found myself at Stockport College, after getting my GCSE's but deciding not to stay on to do A'levels at school. I was playing a game of basketball, *for the first time in my life*, when a gentleman introduced himself as Bill and asked me if I wanted to go for a drink after the basketball session. I was, of course, a bit suspicious, as he was in his forties, but then someone told me he was the men's England coach … and he was sitting next to me … in the gymnasium at Stockport College. "You have the X-factor," he told me, though I had no idea what he was talking about. "You have an ability to see what's going on around you," he said. "You see other people's needs, with a vision of how you can win the game, but you also do it with humility, intelligence and caring. It's something I haven't seen in a long time."

He gave me the opportunity to train with him at the Bobby Charlton camps, and that started the next stage of my unstoppable story, because with his assistance, I became the women's basketball coach, working alongside Bill at the young age of 22.

As a player and coach, I was able to spot talent and help others to enter the world of sport. Back in the early 1990's spotting sporting talent wasn't an 'open and closed' book, if we spotted a really tall person, we would literally go to them and ask, 'do you play basketball?' Funny story: one time, I approached a young lady who was about 6'7" and asked her that question. She replied, '….mmm… do you play miniature golf?' Okay … so I overstepped the boundaries there! Scouting back then was kind of a bravado thing, but we were mostly looking for someone with the X-factor. Someone who was unstoppable – switched on in a way that they could turn their emotional vulnerability into fuel on the basketball court or in life.

If they got knocked over, they would get straight back up. It's an attitude of mind. And we're doing the same with football at the moment; it's a fall down, get back up attitude, but not one without empathy. I was, and still am, looking for that extra 5% or 10% that makes a person something special. And I can see that in them.

I was also able to tap into sport as a funnel for dealing with any issues and problems within their lives. If someone is feeling low, depressed, or has lost direction, then basketball, or sport in general, can help you move your emotions. In basketball, you have to make decisions at phenomenally high speeds, most of them academic, and some of them physical. If you can make those decisions at high speed, you can learn to steer the path of your life as well. I was blessed to be able to help a lot of young people by doing that.

That eventually led me into working with Bill to develop the first BTech sports science, national and higher national diplomas. We wrote all the programmes and won all sorts of awards for what we achieved back then. But as I've said many times, a trophy is a step on the line to the next experiences and growth. It's not the end position. Those courses and assessments have gone on to support thousands of people who study sports science and coaching.

I had my son, at the age of 26, while I was still playing and coaching basketball at a high level. Perhaps, though, I should have looked at his father's head circumference before I decided to go down that path; his head was absolutely huge … and he was going nowhere. It was a difficult birth, with me being in labour for 38 hours. They wanted to do a C-section, but I didn't want to be knocked out for the most important moment of my life. I used my basketball as a way to calm myself, bouncing the ball down the walls, breathing and working through it – I was unstoppable.

When they did take me to theatre, I was in the zone and I'd gone into myself; I'd found a level of stability. I was lying there and all I could think about was that it was three in the morning. I felt like the whole world had stopped because a very natural situation had turned into a very dangerous one for both of us. I took the anaesthetist's mask, and before I knew it, Callum was out. He was okay and I was in recovery. It was because all of the layers I'd built in my resilience that I didn't freak out. It showed me, that no matter what circumstance you may face, whatever event is taking place in your life, there is always a way through. If you can just gather your thoughts, gather your mind, stay calm, and use humour, you can get through anything. Humour is a great outlet for many things. This is a story I use to move me forward and educate others as well.

The word that connects to this is resilience, and through the years, I have been focussing on the definition of resilience. What exactly is it? *It's the capability to withstand or to recover quickly from difficulties, while adapting to adversity.* This is something many people don't understand. When they're hit with situations they haven't experienced before, they're scrambling to gather tools to cope, when in fact, all the tools already exist within them.

Our brain is actually much more adept at dealing with things we have already experienced before. The brain is literally like the black box recorder on an aeroplane. It takes in data and then it spits data out in

48

direct relation to the files it already has stored away. For example, if you've already had a situation in your life and you're hit with something similar again, your brain will bring that up, like little elves through your filing cabinets saying, "what did we do then and what was the outcome? Are we going to do the same this time?" It gives you a chance to reflect, *do I run to the hills or sit still?* It will find the reasoning for action within that file. You can imagine as you get older, layers and layers are built up on similar experiences, which sometimes don't serve you. Sometimes, it is healthier to modify or even delete that file, so the pain doesn't continue to build on those experiences. If we can recognise when a repeated event is triggering us, we can modify the level of pain we experience by understanding it.

However, if it's a new experience, we handle it differently. As mentioned previously, we scramble for tools to find a solution. That's when critical skills can be learned to utilise the tools within us.

I'd like to step in at this point and say please don't shy away from opportunities to go into adverse situations, especially if there is someone there to lead you. Those unstoppable situations will give you strength. They will give you the tools, the resilience, the resistance, the capabilities and the raw factor to handle anything thrown at you. If you can get yourself into situations where you push the line a little bit, then you can get more resilience and increase capability. I have done this all my life, but I've done it naturally. I reminded of a song by *Ellen Johnson,* whose lyrics suggest that if you want to improve your life, you should feel the fear and do it anyway.

However, I need to ask the question, *what is fear?* One acronym is *False Evidence of Actual Reality* but my favourite is *Fuck Everything And Run.* When you get to that point, that's when you know you're growing; when you feel that you need to lock the doors and shut yourself away.

When it comes to personal development and growth, the word journey is used quite a lot, but for me it's an incremental thing. People seem to want to go far forward very quickly, but that's when they get tripped up, or their body and system says *it's too much*. It becomes deeply uncomfortable. For me, it's when there is a level of necessary discomfort that I'm unstoppable. Discomfort can be a very healthy thing. For example, take cold water swimming, you can't just walk into freezing cold water, stay in there for ten minutes and expect to still come out smiling.

I took my Singapore friend, Cindy, for a cold-water swim for the first time. She put her big toe in, screamed, fell over, curled up into the foetal position and said I was crazy. Being from Singapore, she's not experienced temperatures below 28°C so it was a real shock to the system. But we went back, everyday, until one day she had walked in up to her chest, and soon she was immersed in freezing water for three minutes. Her sense of achievement and elation was incredible. For her next challenge, she now knows that small incremental steps lead to success. When Cindy went back to Singapore, her business grew exponentially. She had gained the confidence to take on anything, and everything changed.

Ice is an amazing healing mechanism, it actually hums like a singing bowl. Fast moving water is also very powerful. We often take people through waterfalls, and then straight into cold water. Another way to feel incredibly empowered is to lift heavy stones above your head. Of course, it starts with small increments, one kilogram, three, then five, until you're lifting stones you'd never expect. The roar you let out while lifting the stone is incredible. When you've achieved this, you discover everything is possible. It doesn't matter what words are used on you, what person or situation comes your way, you're able to process things in a way that has nature alongside you.

I've been taking tours to Iceland now, because it's easy to slip into a level of discomfort there. You can be in a hailstorm and then five minutes later, be running away from pure lava, literally flowing down the road. Or suddenly you can have a sandstorm chasing you or be hit by severe snow.

One time I was driving through a snowstorm that was so severe I couldn't see the road in front of me. I also had a responsibility for some quite well-known people in the car as well. I had to stay calm. Because of the skills I've learned, I was able to look serene in very dangerous circumstances. There were cliffs to one side, cars behind and in front so no one could stop and say, *I'll just sit this one out;* we had to get off the mountain. It took 2 hours with me literally driving off the line on the GPS. Eventually, we made it through the storm and off the mountain. My passengers all exclaimed that they could never have done that, but I think in those circumstances you must totally believe in yourself, and you'll discover you are capable – you can achieve anything.

That's not to say that I haven't had my fair share of deeply personal and emotional challenges, indeed, I've hit big challenges, some I haven't been able to handle, some that felt phenomenally unfair and unjust. And they came from nowhere, with no facts, evidence or truth. But for those, you have to sit still and talk it through with the people who support you. If I hadn't had a core inside me and the skills I've learned, which is to get into nature, I may not have handled them in the same way. Just like the crazy Icelandic people, living in a country of fire and ice, nothing waivers them. I sometimes feel I have faced more emotional experiences than many people my age, but I think it may be that I've been put in those positions to enable me to grow further. And in turn, I'm able to help others move out of their emotional and physical pain.

If there is just one thing I could share to help you move forward right now … it's my favourite saying – *This too shall pass!*

If you take on this knowledge with you through any big issues, sit still and reflect – everything will pass. For me, the action happens between the ticking of the clock, the gap between the seconds. That's where the beauty is, where you hit the sweet spots and the peak experiences. Suddenly everything flows.

PAULA ESSON

I am a spirited adventurer, who carves the path of life with resilience and fun. Bringing a vibrant spirit and active lifestyle to my exploration and discoveries.

I bridge my days between Iceland, Northern Ireland and now Glasgow, creating opportunities for women to truly expand their capabilities and potential using the powerful force of nature and the land of Ice and Fire. Often creating limitless possibilities for those that join me and a true sense of personal achievement.

Behind the daring exterior lies a caring and compassionate soul, always ready to lend a helping hand to those in need and as a sport scientist I achieve this through hands on connection, a deep understanding of the body and the energetic link to the experience of pain to create relief and the path to your most creative life.

My journey so far is a testament to the fusion of adventure and empathy, developing strength and balance for people who want to conquer challenges and do so with a heart full of compassion, friendship, and warmth.

I have really created, moved mountains and approached life with a steady resolve, however, I have always stayed grounded in the literal sense, an uncanny knack to really assist people with their endeavours on route to huge successes means that my working career has ranged over the decades from an enthusiastic but naïve basketball coach to reaching the top levels of coaching across many sports and developing the first National and Higher national Diplomas in Sport Science when most people said it would never be possible. In essence, I conjure reality from what doesn't exist yet, and forge opportunities for the future in relation to, not only the young generations but for experienced adults looking for new vibrant pathways. I have created large health centres combining NHS with modern thoughts on health, helped change the landscape of pain management and truly put my heart and soul into reducing the reliance on opioids across the United Kingdom. Presently back working directly in my first love – professional sport, we are now humbly working towards flipping or understanding on how to look after athletes both on and off the field of play, joining the dots properly to prevent injury and take care of the players who are navigating their own journeys'.

I re-set by dedicating myself to my community clinics helping people with the usual aches and pains of life. It truly gives me purpose to know that I can assist people to be at work pain free and give their families and loved ones the best version of themselves.

Paula's website is www.paulaessonclinic.com

Retirement is not a destination in my career... change ...is.
Paula Esson

THE SOUL OF ME
BRIED LYNCH

Now in my sixth decade, I ponder what could possibly be my unstoppable story? Taking the time to consider this, the question that springs to mind is, 'Is the person I believe I am, in my mind, who I actually am?

I could go with the narrative of boring little old me, who has, on balance, enjoyed an absolutely blessed life, but that's not much of an unstoppable story!

In reality, that is not who I am, but it may be the way others perceive me.

I come from a wholesome loving family, have a rock-solid husband, four amazing resilient sons, with extended and blended families of their own. This has given me the privilege of having genuine loving daughters-in-law and happy, fun-loving grandchildren.

Often in life, we judge people on who we see in front of us, who they were five, ten, twenty years ago … or who we perceive them to be. We place our judgement on how they behaved when we knew them, what they wear, who their friends are, where they live, and so on.

But am I the same person I always was? Are my values the same? Do I have the same knowledge I always had, the same circle of friends and associates? Life experiences evolve and change, and with it so did I. I now know who I am and what my unstoppable story is. I invite you to come along for the dander with *Unapologetically Me*.

APOLOGETICALLY ME

Living life by the rules with a good moral compass and a compulsory helping of hard work, I'm known for staying in my lane, taking on everyone else's feelings, thoughts and opinions on every decision I make. Fundamentally, ensuring that I am keeping everyone happy. I don't need to have the final say, compliance is my thing.

A life of no big dramatics, no over-achieving, no merits of distinction here. The only award I received was for politeness and courtesy. Living under the radar, plodding along, fitting in. The reality of my existence is live and let live.

Don't get me wrong I had my adventures and lived a full, happy life which I enjoyed. I especially loved organising and hosting, at work and at home. Give me anything to do for someone else and I will excel at it. The spotlight must always be on someone or something else. I am the background person, living in the wings. I am the doer not the achiever. I am the person shouldering responsibility, taking blame, sorting problems. I am the enabler.

This was Apologetically Me.

The roles we give ourselves and others, how we speak to both, how we are made feel, what we see, especially as young children, have impact. The company we keep, the interactions, the external and peripheral relationships, the noises are all being swallowed into our minds. A little mind without a filter, the early years of life have such significance and impact on who or what we become. As said by the Greek philosopher Aristotle ~ *"Give me the child until he is 7 and I will give you the man."* We can all look back, to acknowledge who we have become.

STOPPABLE ME

A summers day, in the south of France. Sixteen-year-old me, one of a large group of impressionable teenagers and young adults, we had arrived the previous day and were now having the induction of our trip. This was my fourth trip with this amazing organization, so I knew the format of how the days ran. As I contentedly sat in the energy of calmness, I was unaware of the power and impact the words yet to be spoken would affect the happiness and joy I allowed into my life - for the next four decades.

"For the privilege of being chosen to be here, God will ask a lot of you in your life."

This short statement was what my sixteen-year-old self heard, out of everything that was said over the next 90 minutes.

As a teenager brought up to respect my elders, to learn from the learned and a moral compass of belief, I had absolute blind faith and obedience in the teachings of those I was entrusted in the care of. I took these words into my heart, absorbed them into my being and I owned them. I also knew the privilege I had, being there.

These words profoundly affected me from that day forward. For decades, I would awake in the morning and wonder what disaster, tragedy or unfortunate circumstance was going to come into my life.

Despite everything good that happened, I kept believing something bad was coming to take it away. You see that talk, on that Summer's day in1981, was never discussed again; no one gave me any insight into what it meant. I automatically took a negative connotation from it, as I believed I was worthy of having something huge and big happen to me. For me, however, that equated to something big and bad.

This was Stoppable Me.

Words are transformational when we have an audience, whether that is with a child or a conference of thousands. Our words will impact differently for each person receiving them. Whilst we cannot control the way they are heard, we have the power in saying them to control the context. Impressionable people are not just the very young. Be wise with your words.

MY INNER CHILD

Ten years earlier a similar process had occurred that would set the trajectory of limitation on my life. At age six, I can vividly recall being shamed and demoralised by the adult who, at the time, was responsible for me and my education. On the day in question, I was punished for not knowing the correct spelling. My punishment was further verified for me as being what happens for trying, when a more senior adult witnessed and ignored how I was being treated.

Stored in the memory of my subconscious mind for fifty plus years, was the belief that it is not safe to try; to answer out incorrectly is a punishable behaviour. I sat throughout my education being the quiet one at the back of the class, never connecting, always believing that learning had no real benefit for me. To fail was better than to try. If I didn't try, I would be safe. To hold the *failure I was inside* was all I knew how to do. In the 70s, children were seen and not heard.

The only time I found this not to be true was when I had the lovely Lucy as my guardian in class. Throughout my life and to this day, I have a soul connection with this beautiful lady who regularly shows up in my thoughts and in spirit connection.

As an adult, I still tremble to speak out loud in a group. It can be with family, strangers or friends I have yet to meet - the overwhelm is real. The sweating, the shaking voice the memory blank and the words no one can hear or understand. This is still a thing in my life…. but it only affects the topic of Me. I can speak for and about anyone else with conviction and strength, but not for or about the person I should love the most.

Strange to say, I felt so connected to my sons that I could seldom use my voice for them. In my subconscious, they were an extension of me and I was as unable to speak for them as I was for myself. The profound effect of losing my voice rolled over into the next generation, not by genes, but by belief. Fortunately for them, they had a father who was confident in who he was and had enough belief in himself, me and the family to allow us to use his belief in us, until we finally found belief in ourselves.

Over the last few years, this has been a statement I have been given often: *Borrow the belief I have in you, until you get your own.* I loved this and have used others belief in me on occasion. However, long term this didn't work for me. Now I am able to use the power of changing the belief that I hold subconsciously, process through it, and change the belief to one I consciously want.

Inside each of us is our inner child; that part of our subconscious that experienced and still remembers those feelings and emotions of our formative years. Today we have the phenomenal ability and knowledge to tap into the subconscious mind, allowing us to get directly to the emotional triggers we absorbed in our young formative years. The young inner child can be loved by the older you and set free.

THE CONSCIOUS ME

Living consciously is where we ideally want to be, but as noted by the renowned Dr Joe Dispenza, we spend 95% of our lives living in our subconscious, as he discusses in his book *You Are The Placebo,* and helps change in *Breaking The Habit of Being Yourself.* He is an amazing authority on the power of our subconscious mind.

I was previously oblivious to the impact of what is stored in my subconscious mind. The awareness of what is there, why it is there and how it affects me, only came to light when I went on the journey of personal development.

Educating myself with the works of great authors, including Dr Joseph Murphy and Dr Bruce Lipton, and continuing to study metaphysical anatomy, I am gaining wisdom I can use to empower myself and release the attachment of needing to be something or someone my subconscious believes I should be. My subconscious, working away to keep me safe from dangerous situations, triggers the feelings I store, then draws on them when the same emotional response is triggered in my life today. In the reality of my life now, I more and more often live from a place of consciousness, a place of awareness. Having the fulfilment of my self-healing journey and daily sessions reaching into my subconscious mind, through the use of Belief Coding®, my days mostly evolve on a different vibration.

My destiny has been found through the deep diving journey into *letting go* of the over-thinking, people pleasing, judgement, dependable person I always made myself for others. They did not put this expectation on me … I did. I volunteered to always be available by not saying 'No.' I volunteered by always changing my plans to fit in with the narrative. I volunteered by not taking responsibility that I was a person too. I had a voice but my subconscious had taken it away to keep me safe, years previously. Our subconscious' job is to keep us safe but at what cost… Radical responsibility changes all this.

Being consciously aware of my thoughts, my words, my actions, my habits, values and my destiny, enables me to turn the narrative on its head; to be in the driving seat of my destiny. It presents me with uplifting days, as I use my awareness from dawn to dusk. I see the vibrancy in the day, in my life, in the lives of others. Everything shows up in techno-colour, just how consciously-me can become Unstoppable Me.

THE ANGELS AND ME

As an adult of 21, I returned to the South of France. The difference was profound.

I had the freedom to sit in the absolute wonder, silence and the presence of something so much greater than I am. The quiet stillness of my own presence in one of the most sacred energetic spaces I have ever known.

The oneness, the grounded sensation, the belonging, the knowing. I feel fulfilled, in awe of the greatness of our universe, the complete faith in the wonder and splendour of a power so vast, so spectacular, but so individual, that I have a personal connection that is eternal, infinite. I sit experiencing the wrapping of the spirit around me.

From this day forwards, I use the angels more intensely in every situation in everyday life guiding, directing, surrounding, protecting. I use them to help everyone I know and anyone I'm guided to, even when I don't know them. The angels have no limits, so I put no limits on who they help, all they ever need is to be invited in.

I always assumed everyone used the angels every day. I had no concept I was different, that it wasn't a thing! This realisation came 35 years later.

The important thing with the angels is, when you call on them, they always answer. But like us humans, they like to be thanked.

THE INVISIBLE ME

It was a Friday in February when my mental health took a nosedive, the day that was to be the end of the life I had known for almost 30 years. Thirty years of striving, building, sacrificing, growing, achieving, succeeding, of ups and downs, but a life I believed would *always be.*

Not so. My life irrevocably changed, affecting not only myself, but the lives of every member of my family, my friends, my colleagues, the business and the community, with a ripple effect throughout the region.

Administration is an ordinary word; easy to say, easy to spell, doesn't cause earthquakes, it's no big deal. Unless you are going through it … not an earthquake but definitely quicksand with an express train charging onwards overhead.

The quicksand is swallowing up everything in its path; community, self-worth, value, ability, communication, involvement, belonging, appreciation, trust, loyalty, resilience. Whilst on the train above, it's a completely different world; the excitement the thrill of the station master and the guards on board tripping over themselves at the elation of the glory of the prize.

Breaking the pieces of what once was my life, as I saw it, into chunks to fit into the carriages they brought along, to make it disappear, unvaluable and nonexistent. And so it is…. thirty years of life gone in less than 90 seconds.

The black hole I found myself in got deeper and darker. I no longer had the ability to feel! Numbed to the core, I wasn't a wife, a mother, a daughter, a sister, a grandmother, a friend, a me. I was nothing. I was no one. Physically, emotionally, mentally and spiritually depleted.

I had failed. The despair of loss was profound, overwhelming. The fall out and backlash of being a part of an administration was crushing. I was a nervous wreck, heartbroken and with a heart ache that would not lift. One day, a counsellor suggested I treat it like grief, but not as one loss but as a loss of all the individual parts … the business, the family, the community, the job, the jobs of my family members, the home, the possessions, the family's homes, then all the emotional factors attached to the individual losses. That was huge. The black abyss was real.

I became invisibly me.

I existed, barely. I had mind gremlins who tortured me, but I became an expert at numbing them. I spent my days alone, empty, a vessel of despair. I lost sight of myself and everyone I cared about. Once a week I had a reprieve, as I had one person to care about, and that gave me a reason to be. The gratitude I hold for this blessing goes deep for me; she was my lifeline.

In life and times of darkness, our trials or demons can be broken down into bite-size chunks. Acknowledge how they make us feel individually. Seeking out the help we need is so far out of our capability. Until we can get to that point, accept the help of anyone who reaches out. Respond and acknowledge people who care as they will be your lifeline. The friend (Roisin) who calls you and tells you to put on the music and dance doing the housework, is the one you want to call even when you haven't washed your face in a week and there is no housework as your bed is the only space you inhabit. Just put the music on. Gradually over time those minutes of music grow until you actually hear it.

It's all an *Inside Job*

Fast forward to 2019, once more I'm back in the South of France. This time alone, as one solo part of a bigger group of whom I know no one, and could continue to be invisibly me, in a place that brought me complete happiness.

An inclusive invitation from two ladies, Eleanor and Mary, paved the path of the rest of my life, the transformation to the Unstoppable Me.

It is no coincidence I am back in the place where I have my greatest spiritual attachment to meet these beautiful souls. A place where I feel the most grounded, connected, aware of my own sense of being.

When we find this kind of peace and connection to ourselves, we should sit with it, absorb it and realise that this is how we want to be every day. This is something that is available to us wherever we are, not just in one location where we feel the pull and draw to on Earth.

We hold within us the realisation that it's "all an inside job." Y, We bring this with us wherever we go, whatever we do. It is our soul connection, our spirit, our *all-knowing*.

If only I had the wisdom forty years, even twenty years earlier that I had this complete connection within.

THE UNAPOLOGETIC ME

Within a few weeks of arriving home, I shed so much of the un-living I was doing.

I was making new connections, step after step, I started to live again. The fog had lifted. I met amazing new people, each in their own way adding to my life, and my sense of wellness and growth.

Reading and listening, getting absorbed into the positive transformational success stories of others, I began to regain confidence. Getting back to volunteering, which I loved, was by no coincidence, setting me up for a different type of connecting. Rambling, sea-dipping, book clubs, fitness classes, socialising groups and attending networking events; the alignment to my life purpose was evolving.

The last quarter of 2021 was to be the most transformational, when I started working with my intuitive mentor. Geraldine opened my eyes to the ability to see what could actually become my reality. Trusting my own intuition, my gut and going for what I loved, and quite naturally was good at, was the most amazing experience. I was trusting myself, opening up to being unapologetically me and working harder on myself than anything else. I became selfless, in that I gave *me* the time and love I needed to become the best I could be.

THE UNSTOPPABLE ME!

My growth and direction came with changes to the way I live my life day to day. I am so fortunate I have a whole new community of like-minded supportive people. Every day is a new adventure, where I get to prioritise me, so I can be the best for my clients and those in my life. I accept radical responsibility for my decisions.

There are challenges along the way as there always will be. The difference is the response to these challenges.

Challenges I now work through by going inwards and by using the masterful energy of the angels. When your co-workers are the angels, you know you have hit the jackpot. The working day just hits differently. Positivity is the vibe, support is continual, carrying your workload is lighter, brighter. A greater vibration than you fills your world, it pushes you to step up and keep stretching your limits to be the Unstoppable Me I was born to be.

In a world where self-awareness, health and our soul-selfs, (as opposed to our sole selfs) are becoming more important, we want to take on the responsibility for keeping our energy positive. We want to consciously live our best life. Life is a journey not a destination and we evolve every single day. Every day is a new chance to begin again, and most of all there is no age limit to starting over. Great if you are younger to get ahead sooner, but open your heart, your mind and your soul at any age.

TRANSFORMING ME

Yesterday is history. Tomorrow is a mystery. Today is a gift – that's why we call it 'the present'. ~ Eleanor Roosevelt.

For me living each day in the present with a focus, a knowing, and being open to asking "how can I serve today?" is transformational.

It takes a toolkit to do it and in my daily toolkit is TIME...

To journal (Letting go)

To meditate (Listening)To pray (Asking)To walk (Mindful)To read (Learning)

For gratitude (Appreciation)

I have found the greatest gift so far is the realisation that there is complete freedom to choose. When we make the right choices, we are all Unstoppable.

I am radically responsible for me and me alone. I am able to feel how I want to feel, be how I want to be. I understand no one else can put a feeling on me unless I am willing to accept it. Anger, blame, guilt, shame, judgement, fear, stress, mistrust - I decide if I let these visit with me. I am human, so they still knock on the door, but I have the tools to immediately work on them and release, renew and rebalance my energy, my beliefs. We all have the ability to do this, to avail of this not as an alternative route to health, but embracing it as important as getting our hair done, looking after our skin or whatever we individually do for our health and wealth. We have all heard the saying, 'we glow from the inside out.' I know this to be true, as you can put anything on the outside but it cannot change what is within.

It's all an inside job. We all have the freedon of belief.

BRIED LYNCH

Bried Lynch is a Holistic Entrepreneur. She has a complete joy and delight in using her gifts and skills everyday to show up proudly and unapologetically to transform life's one heart and one belief at a time.

Working as an IET® Master Instructor specialising in facilitating clients with the energy of the angelic realm. Her co-workers are angels and she gets to work with them every day. Bried also trains people to master their own energy through group sessions. Coaching children as well as adults to "get the issues out of their tissues " for good.

She further enhances her offering with empowerment sessions carried out for families, groups or gatherings of 2 -20 people, currently primarily requested for weddings, funerals or team sports.

She loves working with her clients who have an awareness that the stuck, stagnant, blocked energy that they feel within can be released, renewed and rebalanced to bring about the life of their dreams. Clients who journey with her can process right through to bringing forth the manifestation of their life's mission and souls purpose by doing the inner work at cellular level. A gentle, calm non invasive means of servicing the inner energy that drives our bodies not only at every day level but at soul level. It's all an inside job and when we keep the energy flowing life flows with it.

Bried also works as a Belief Coding® Master Facilitator and Inner Freedom coach. Belief Coding® transforms life's by working with the sub conscious mind to get to the root of where the limiting beliefs that show up in our life's come from, process through them and create new beliefs that positively impact us to move forwards.

The issues that show up as trauma, illness, fears, pain, addictions or limits that hold us back are safely, simply and effectively worked on changing the world one belief at a time.

Bried works in person and remotely and facilitates 1 to 1 clients alongside hosting group sessions. With the flexibility around how and where she works she has the ability to work locally and globally enabling transformation in a time efficient manner.

Bried also works as an intuitive, connecting with spirit. She has recently started this journey and continues to hone her skills through training and mentorship. She is throughly enjoying the process and looks forward to where it leads.

Bried has recently started actively seeking opportunities for spreading the awareness and scope of bringing these amazing modalities to the grass roots level. To bring it to children, where it can have impact through their knowledge, understanding and experiencing of how energy and beliefs impacts their life's. To do this I advocate to the Mums, Dads, Grandparents, Aunts, Uncles, Sisters, Brothers, Cousins, Friends who read this today to get in touch to see how you can help. Firstly for yourself so you can be a part of your inner healing, then to ensure that one small person you know gets the opportunity to transform their own life. How precious and important would that one small step be for a child to be acknowledged for their capabilities to understand energies and the ability to change beliefs as life progresses. Prevention rather than cure holistically.

Bried's Instagram is www.instagram.com/briedlynch

THE POWER OF PLATINUM
JENNY GORDON

When I was a little girl, I wanted to be a hairdresser. I loved watching the stylists do their thing, although this was long before the days of celebrity hairdressers, other than Vidal Sassoon (1928 -2012). I loved the space they created, the glossy magazines, the mirrors, the music, the chat, a veritable oasis for women. It always seemed to me that they left with more sashay in their step, walking taller and with more confidence than when they arrived. Having attempted to test my talents on my dolls hair with decidedly wonky results, I considered that perhaps I was destined for another career. However, my love of hairdressing remains to this day and I have never forgotten the positive impact of a great haircut; not simply the physical beauty, but the energetic beauty of connecting to the power inside.

I was very proud of my dark brown hair. I was determined to keep it, so when I started to go grey in my thirties, I dabbled with home dye kits, and when it became tricky, I sought professional help. I succumbed to the societal conditioning that *grey is distinguished in men and ageing in women*, and so began my thirty-year relationship with the permanent dye bottle. That opinion was so entrenched in society, that not only did I not challenge it, I also actively encouraged it in myself and others; the myth was perpetuated in my belief system. 'Don't make me look

Mumsy' was a regular request to my hairdresser who, having been trained by Vidal Sassoon, was only too happy to oblige. When my eldest son was approaching his thirtieth birthday, he said to me, 'I remember you being thirty Mum and thinking it was completely ancient. Of course, now I am thirty, I realise it is no age at all!' Ageism is alive and well, and the reason it feels important to make it the focus of this chapter, is because it buries brilliance by attempting to dim our light.

There is a constant call to fit in to a particular image, a pressure to be all things to all people at the same time, with the implicit threat that if you do not manage to stay young looking, you will find yourself discarded and of little use to the world. I read a letter in the SAGA magazine recently; an excellent magazine aimed at the over 50s. The letter was from a woman who shared her experience of 'going grey', having stopped dying her hair. Since doing so, she said she had become invisible, was spoken to slowly and loudly in case she was hard of hearing as well as grey, and generally felt unseen, unheard and thoroughly miserable. So much so, she was heading back to her hairdressers to become a blonde! Ageism is still alive and kicking. I submitted a reply, offering an alternative perspective which I am delighted to say, they published.

When I left school, a career often meant having the same job for all your working life. I trained as a general and sick children's nurse because it had the potential for me to work anywhere in the world. It was a fabulous career, and I loved all the roles I had. When I found myself unexpectedly out of a job at fifty, I stood on the pavement in London, clutching the contents of my office in a cardboard box. A large part of me was terrified I would never find another job because of my age, and a tiny part was excited about the possibilities… *what if this was my moment to do something wildly different?*

I found a great coach, and as a qualified coach myself, I knew what I needed. He looked at my CV and asked if I had ever considered a portfolio career. He said he saw evidence of an entrepreneurial spirit and many transferrable skills that would serve me well. I replied that I had considered it, but thought I was way too old to start from scratch. 'It's time to act your age Jenny,' he said, 'the right clients will see your wisdom, experience and gravitas. What's stopping you?'

That was a great question. It felt like a big ask, it felt scary, and I wasn't sure I could do it. I thought of a thousand reasons why it may not work. I checked out lots of job boards and didn't love any of the roles on offer enough to apply. The 'unstoppable' seed had been sown and had started to take root. Slowly but surely, the belief in my potential to have a new career in the second half of my life grew. I reconnected with my purpose to help others to see the brilliance they had buried within. I discovered the work of Dr Clarissa Pinkola Estes who writes so eloquently of becoming an elder, and of late bloomers. I read avidly and took inspiration from her. It wasn't long before *Jenuine Consulting Ltd* became a reality.

Wisdom can be a tricky balance; sharing what you know and making it relevant and accessible to those you are working with. We are much more likely to accept shared wisdom when it comes from a credible and trusted source; someone we can identify with, someone who has had their fair share of challenges. Like many other professionals, I have spent years collecting qualifications, continually learning from courses and experience, practising and making mistakes and learning some more. I have come a long way from my one wonky attempt as a hairstylist. I know that wisdom is a lifelong endeavour, that enlightenment takes repeated immersion in the learning, going deeper each time, and that age is a privilege denied to many. Over the years, my business has evolved as I have worked on my own self-awareness and self-development so that I can better serve others.

I have broken through many of my life limiting beliefs, but the belief that *grey hair is ageing* was deeply entrenched. I was liberated, albeit reluctantly after lockdown, emerging skunk like once my beloved hairdresser re-opened. She tentatively suggested the colour underneath the dark brown was beautiful, and surely, I had noticed the trend for young people to colour their hair grey/silver/platinum. I muttered about the fact that it may be *cool to dye your hair grey when you are young, but I suspected it was less cool when you are older.* She suggested I give it a try and if I really hated the result, I could always return to being a brunette. I decided I couldn't wait for the remaining dark to grow out, so I booked a very long appointment, where the colour was chemically removed, and I left embracing my new natural platinum. Perhaps I'm not always as patient as I would like to believe.

It was a bit of a shock and it took some getting used to. At first it didn't feel like me. I surprised myself many times in the mirror, wondering who the person staring back at me was. It took time to own it and with that ownership came increased confidence, a sense of freedom and the feeling that I had a deeper connection with my true purpose. My hair is now naturally more than 50 shades of grey and I choose to refer to it as Platinum because it's a brilliant analogy for how I show up in the world.

Platinum is an incredibly rare and precious metal with plenty of unique qualities. It is extremely durable, resistant to corrosion and tarnish, and its high density means it's also resistant to wear and tear. This could be wishful thinking on my part perhaps. The human equivalent is resilience, the ability to navigate the ups and downs of life, and there are plenty of those, sometimes arriving out of the blue in huge waves. How do we stop ourselves from being swamped?

I am a naturally positive person and have a daily gratitude practice. Every morning before I get out of bed, I think of five things I am grateful for. Sometimes they are big things, but often they are the small simple things it can be easy to forget. When I get into the shower, I choose my attitude for the day - a habit I learned from Debra Searle MVO MBE, a professional adventurer and serial entrepreneur; another unstoppable woman. I think in the spirit of fairness, I should point out that on good days, my attitude lasts all day, and on some days, I am lucky to make it to lunch time. I like to keep it real. We all have days where we aren't on top form and the ability to acknowledge this without shame is an important facet of brilliance.

Platinum is chemically inert. I last did chemistry at university, so it's been a while. Chemically inert means it is incredibly stable and doesn't react with other chemicals. This can come in very useful in relationships, both business and personal. Relationships that work well are those where we choose to respond rather than react. This is one example of how understanding personality traits comes into its own. We all have traits, strengths and preferences that prompt our behaviours. We often assume others have the same ones as we do, and that therefore they will share our perspective, only to find that they don't. When we react, we are usually coming from a place of fear (each of us has our own triggers that activate those fears) and when this happens, we are reacting, not from our strengths and preferences, but from our vulnerabilities. Our vulnerabilities are an exaggerated version of those strengths and preferences, so they are experienced as extreme. I am a natural people pleaser. I like it when everyone's needs are being met and I like to help make that happen. My greatest fear is that my help, and I, will be rejected. When this is triggered, my people pleasing preference is taken to the outer limit. I can go to endless lengths, trying to please everyone, compromising to such an extent that my own needs are lost completely. And I become exhausted in the process. I often then feel resentful and unappreciated, as I am the one doing all the giving. Does that sound familiar? Once I understood this personality trait, I was able to acknowledge and appreciate the strengths of it, accepting that when my fear is triggered, it creates a vulnerability that doesn't serve me or my relationships. I have worked hard to explore the origins of those triggers. These will be different for each of us, even though we may share the same personality trait because we will all have had life experiences. Now I know what my triggers are, I can (mostly) interrupt the pattern and notice what's coming up for me so that I choose to respond from a place of strength, rather than react from a place of vulnerability. This process has had such a positive impact on all my relationships.

You may think that may sound a bit 'cold' and calculating for some-one who loves connectivity and interaction, but fear not - platinum is a brilliant conductor of electricity ... so the spark we feel is real. As I have gotten older, I have reclaimed the energetic connection I had as a child; the energetic connection I believe we are all born with. Some may call it intuition, and it is often buried deep down, out of sight and out of mind. For me, it's now out in the open, and it brings me much joy and insight.

Platinum has a high melting point. In my case, I like to think I'm incredibly patient most of the time, with an ability to appreciate multi-ple perspectives. However, do not mistake this for a lack of boundaries or the ability to make difficult decisions when required. Many people, including several of my clients, have been burned by various psychomet-ric testing and personality assessments, of which there are many. They say they feel they have been 'put into a box' and I've encountered responses like 'don't ask me to do any detail, I am an ENFP.' The assessment can be used as a reason to stagnate.

As with any tool, it's the way you use them that matters. We can, of course, access any trait we choose; it just takes more energy and focus to access those that are not our favourites. We are multifaceted human beings with the capacity to become whoever we wish to be. When a lap-idarist cuts and polishes precious gems, they do so in a way that brings out the best in each individual stone, using both light and dark to max-imise its sparkle. In the same way, I help my clients to reclaim and buff their brilliance by exploring and understanding the many facets of their personalities in ways that work for them.

Platinum has the most beautiful lustre, a gentle, bright, luminescent quality, highly attractive to others. My mission is to change the way we think about ageing. I celebrate that young people are choosing to dye their hair grey; I celebrate that they are no longer tied to the soul shrivelling belief that grey hair is ageing and, that if you are old, you are of limited use. We are living longer and with the ever-changing world of technology, we have the capacity to make positive contributions at any age, any time, any place - to misquote the original Martini advert!

To become an elder is a precious gift, owning our wisdom and our wild souls. We were born within us, all we need to do our work; to take our place in the lives we choose to live. As Dr Clarissa Pinkola Estes reminds us, 'Now is the just-right time, like Sleeping Beauty, to break the enchantment, to truly awaken and awaken others, as either a rookie Dangerous Old Woman, a mid-career Dangerous Old Woman, or as Crone with crown complete.'

People sometimes ask why I use *Dr* as my title. The simple answer, is that I earned it through studying my PhD. The second, is that it serves as a daily reminder that I am also a Dangerous Old Crone, incredibly proud of the unstoppable power of platinum.

I'm not sure if my crown is yet complete, and I am looking forward to the next stage of my mission. I hope this story has inspired you, whatever your age. We each bloom in are own time and some of us are destined to bloom many times over. I believe you get to choose and that your unique brilliance will guide you. Take time to enjoy exploring, and remember, you are never alone - others have walked the paths before you.

JENNY GORDON

J enny is based in Oxfordshire, serving the world. I am a work in progress. Powered by JENERGY ... the essence of my unique brilliance and Whole-being! I use mine to activate yours. Mum, Nanny, Aunt, Cousin, Friend, Confidante, embracing the Dangerous Old Crone phase of my life with joy, passion and purpose so much still to be and do.

I am a personality trait specialist, and business/life and leadership coach with a background in health, paediatrics was my specialist area. Using my considerable life experience, scientific background together with my doctoral expertise that brings a wealth of insight that I have used in a variety of sectors including engineering, finance, healthcare, retail and education every day to stimulate my own and others thinking.

My preference is to use collaborative approaches to translate vision into reality, helping people to rediscover, reconnect with and develop their potential and their influence by understanding themselves so that they can share their unique brilliance in all spheres of their lives.

'You can't go back and change the beginning, but you can start where you are and change the ending' C.S. Lewis

Jenny's LinkedIn is www.linkedin.com/in/jenuineconsulting

THE AWAKENED DREAMER WHO DARED TO BELIEVE IN HERSELF
ROSIE KEANEY

D o you ever feel like you want to scream, that you want to shout but the words just won't come out!

That's exactly how I've felt during various stages of my life. There was so much I wanted to say but it's like I was on mute; the words would run away from me when I needed them the most. The times when I would eventually summon up the courage to speak my truth, my words would be completely misunderstood.

It was a beautiful crisp Spring day and I was travelling to Manchester with my mum and my sister, Geraldine, for an event I'd been dreaming of for the previous six months. This was a huge step for me. After four years of not valuing my individual contribution to the world, I was going to be participating at an event where successful and confident people resided; a place I could never have imagined twelve months before.

The event was called *Be Inspired*. It was held at a Manchester United Football stadium, ironically or not, in the *Theatre of Dreams*. This was my first sign. From the moment we landed in Manchester that weekend,

I knew I was in the right timeline. The signs came thick and fast. As I entered the building, I was greeted with a *Hello Sausage* banner; a large graphic printed on the wall of the stadium. My sister, Dean, has been calling my five-year-old son *Sausage* since the day he was born! Every step I took, I was met with more and more inspiration; words with meaning, powerful quotes and visuals all affirming I was in the right place.

This was my once-in-a-lifetime opportunity to live my dream, to be who I really wanted to be. Nobody knew me here, other than my sister, so there was no judgement, no awareness of my past experiences, only the most amazing opportunity to be my true self. This was both terrifying and extremely liberating.

I felt like Alice in Wonderland, there was so much to explore. There was no dress code; people dressed as their true selves, the more flamboyant the better. I was back to the old me in my sparkles and glamour. It was everything I had dreamed of, as if I'd stepped back in time to my youth. It was only six months earlier when my sister had told me about this event and I wasn't even sure back there if I should go. Procrastination was my best friend. I had questioned whether or not I should be a part of this many times, however being there confirmed I had found my people. I was in the right place at the right time, even though I was completely out of my comfort zone. Interestingly though, so was everyone else. It was a wonderful feeling and I was beaming like a Cheshire cat. Surely I am entitled to live my dreams, right?

Towards the end of day two, the event was wrapping up for an after-party and I found myself surrounded by some of the incredible speakers and organisers of the event. My sister, Geraldine, had some networking to do and suddenly, my palms were sweaty, my heart was racing and I didn't know how to communicate. I was comparing myself to everyone else in the room and I started to feel as if the room was spinning. I didn't feel like I had anything important to say, *why would anyone listen to me?* My anxiety levels started to run through the roof. I started to panic, my thoughts had catastrophised and I was beginning to feel out of my depth. I took myself out of the room to breathe, to just be with my own thoughts, and I had the realisation that I didn't need to *people please* to fit in; I just needed to be me. Wow! What a revelation. I didn't need to put on a big façade. In that very moment the energy shifted for me; I had finally and willingly accepted *me*!

In 2018, as a forty-year-old mum of four, I had put my life on pause. I had closed the doors to my business overnight and it was one of the most difficult decisions I'd ever made in my life. I was in the spotlight for all the wrong reasons. This was not good for my self-esteem; I felt like an outcast and was publicly humiliated. I let people down, which absolutely devastated me.

What I did not realise at the time, was that the business closure and the years leading up to that experience, were due to trauma and the PTSD I was experiencing. I had become overly anxious, while my self-esteem and confidence had nosedived. I no longer recognised myself in the mirror - nor did I want to. It wasn't until several years later that I had an epiphany, realising that my breakdown had led me to my *breakthrough*.

As a youngster I was a control freak, and still to this day I can be triggered by the fear of the unknown and fear of not being accepted. Subconsciously, I had these feelings throughout my life. They had always been there, but they were buried deep down, suppressed, dormant for so many years. In 2018, they had risen to the surface enough for shockwaves to rock my world. So much so, that I would have no choice but to stop and listen to my inner, most hidden emotions and fears, as well as my intuition. It was time for me to do the work; to start my self-healing journey, with the assistance of the spirit world and some incredible humans too.

All my life I've been a dreamer. I could easily switch worlds in an instant. With the click of my fingers I would be transported to my imaginary world……my imagination. Everything there was perfect, full of awe and wonder. It was forgiving, loving and kind, whereas the real world often felt overwhelming to me; it felt sad, unhappy and too difficult to face at times.

As a young child, my family would often joke; *Rosie is dreaming again.* Little did they, or I, even realise I was in another world, or that I had a powerful connection with the spirit world. I vividly remember my happiest memories would be when I was playing alone. Whether that was playing with my dolls house or walking around an enchanted outdoor space, my imagination ran wild. I was often drawn to sacred buildings, hosting a variety of mystical symbols, fountains, and historical graves.

Through my connection to nature, spirit and my childlike wonder, everything was beautiful. I would happily play and communicate with my spirit guides (as I know now), for hours upon end.

My first experience of MAGIC was at the age of five when mum had taken me and my younger sisters to the pantomime for the very first time. My cheeks were flushed with pure excitement and the adrenaline was rushing through my veins. Getting to see theatre and watching fairy tales being played on stage, all of my dreams came true watching real fairy princess in *Cinderella.*

My love for theatre was always there and this continued in my teenage years where I experienced a production of *Joesph And His Technicolour Dream Coat* in Dublin. I was fourteen at the time and remember being captivated and transported to the land of dreams.

As I grew older, I became detached from my dream like qualities, fearful of retribution from my teachers, in case I drifted into my dream world at school. I was afraid of being asked a question and not knowing the answer, due to being so easily distracted. This often did lead to embarrassment in front of my peers, so I strived to become less of the dreamer I loved to be, even though this was where I felt my most happiest, content and accepted.

Throughout my teenage years I was carefree, everything was *Rosey,* however my innocent nature began to be perceived by others as gullible or easily deceived, rather than my inner goodness. This, in turn, silenced my voice due to fear of rejection and not fitting in or being accepted for who I truly was.

As the years progressed, I became more of a people pleaser, silently losing my true self. The emotional pain I was feeling felt like a boulder I was carrying around at times. I would try to supress my emotions and lock them away in the hope they would disappear. But they didn't vanish, they had a habit of showing up when I least expected, often resulting in me not knowing how to self-regulate, which would then result in emotional outbursts.

I was always questioning, why didn't I fit in and why the prettiest girl was chosen, over me, to do a dance act I'd been practicing for a whole month. These small negative experiences of rejection were being subconsciously banked, adding to my limiting beliefs slowly increasing as I grew up.

The very first CD I brought, at the age of 13, was *Heal The World* by Michael Jackson. I would play it on repeat, always believing in the goodness in the world and how everyone has kindness within them. , however, this belief was constantly challenged by what was happening in the real world around me.

Throughout my teenage years I was constantly questioning myself around what life was about and how we exist, and even breathe. I started to think there was something wrong with me. How could the world be so good when it was so wrong? How could my beliefs about kindness make a difference when I was only one small fish in a great big ocean? I was becoming undone.

Entering early adulthood, I became susceptible to my people pleasing tactics, just to try and fit in. I truly felt I couldn't be myself; I had to blend in. As I didn't go to university, until I was in my thirties so conversations would confuse me. I didn't contribute as I believed I wasn't academic or smart enough. However, talk to me about beauty or spiritu-ality and I would be engrossed; I could talk all day about these topics. I actually believed *I was weird*.

My disconnect often manifested as anger, frustration and judgment because I was so unhappy within myself. I began to focus on the weak-nesses of others, and myself, as opposed to the positives. This led me down a path of self-destruction, being unkind to myself, and even to others at times, not realising the emotional damage this would cause to the people I truly cared about.

I was frustrated. I felt silenced. I felt that if I wasn't in the room, no one would even notice I wasn't there. There were others who were much more fun and flamboyant than plain old me. What did I have to offer? I wasn't as interesting as the people who surrounded me. I was too serious, too responsible to let my hair down and have fun. I was unable to be carefree.

My journey of self-discovery has made me consciously aware of my limiting beliefs, and how the times I was feeling unloved within myself made it impossible to show love for others. I didn't value my strengths and the contribution I was making in the world, so how could anyone else value me. I finally understood that the lack of love for myself, was a direct correlation of what I was receiving in my friendships and relation-ships; I needed to love me first.

Spirit has always shown me the power of unconditional love. I knew this from a young age, as I could feel it and believe it, but it took until my later years to believe in my own inner magic, or to set myself free from the fears of what I perceived others thought of me. The most powerful experience was when I started to focus on my self-discovery and personal development journey. As the dots joined together, I starting to put my mediumship practises into play, as I had forgotten during my later teen-age years and early adulthood what this truly felt like.

From my breakdown in 2018, I started to uncover parts of me I had forgotten. The more I delved into the journey through the pain barriers, the fears, the hardships, the overwhelming emotions and the tears, the more I reignited a burning passion within me, each elevation returning me closer to my soul, my dreamer, my dancer and my free spirit; my soul, my writer.

Throughout my life the right people would always show up for me. Do you recall similar experiences where the this has happened to you? There is always a reason, a season or a lifetime for a person entering your world. Sometimes they borrow you their belief in you until you learn to love yourself – it's so powerful!

Here are my top tips for starting a spiritual journey:

Self-love – It is critically important that you learn to love yourself; your darkness and your light. You are here for a purpose, so become your number one fan!

Self-worth – We are all worthy of love, we are all worthy of opportunity, we are all worthy of abundance in every area of our life - you just need to believe it too.

Self-compassion – The most important person to be kind to you, is you. You deserve to be treated respectfully and nurtured to your full potential. Learn to become consciously aware of your unkind words … and reprogramme them subconsciously.

Self-forgiveness - The power in letting go. Failure is not the end, failure is only the beginning. It is an opportunity to learn and grow. Don't allow your mistakes to become your burdens, let them go and set yourself free with forgiveness.

Self-coaching - Allow yourself to be coached. Your body knows the score. You need to listen to your inner knowing as your intuition will guide you onto the right path. There are no wrong decisions in life, only opportunities . Open up to the endless possibilities available to you.

Dreaming – Your imagination is your unique gift, so allow yourself to dream, as you did as a child. You may find some of those dreams can be repurposed and recreated in your later years. Always believe in your dreams.

ROSIE KEANEY

I'm a Dreamer / Event Host / Project Manager / Author / Intuitive Business Coach / Entrepreneur/ Ted X Speaker /Motivational & Inspirational Speaker

Rosie Keaney a married mum of four has found her purpose in life through the breakdown her business in 2018 she has found her breakthrough and is now on a mission to help others find their true purpose in life through her motivational speaking and events by showcasing the best speakers international and local Speakers in personal development and transformation.

Rosie Keaney a skilled Business and Life coach with a unique specialisation in mediumship. With a passion for helping individuals find balance, clarity and purpose, Rosie combines traditional coaching techniques with a deep connection to the spiritual realm through personalised guidance.

Rosie empowers clients to navigate both professional and personal growth whilst tapping into their intuitive abilities. With a proven track record of fostering success and personal transformation, Rosie is dedicated towards a harmonious integration of your spiritual and business journeys.

For Rosie, there are no limitations in life. Rosie will give advice on how to reach beyond those limitations and how to find your true purpose in life and follow your dreams. After working with Rosie, you allow yourself to shed limiting self-beliefs and give yourself grace to dream big!

Rosie's website is www.dreamerskingdom.co.uk

WOMEN ARE THE
SECRET KEEPERS

VICKY BLADES

Valentine's Day 2017; I remember it well. On a dark and rainy night, I'm climbing the stairs of an old Victorian building. It seems a long way up. My memory is of an attic room at the top of the house, but perhaps I'm being romantic. In any case, it's about 6pm and I have an appointment with Vanessa, one of the counsellors from Nexus NI, the charity for survivors of sexual abuse, violence or rape.

It's a preliminary chat to see if they can help me. You see, I tell Vanessa, "I think I was raped. At uni. Thirty years ago. But I can't be sure …"

And so, it begins.

For the first time in 30 years, I break my silence and tell my allotted therapist all about it. The secret I've kept for all these years is spilling out, and all the usual waves of regret, denial, shame, anger and grief wash over me, in our weekly sessions.

"But what if I got it wrong?" I say. My therapist fixes me with a steely eye.

"Have you?" she says.

No. The-body-keeps-the-score. I haven't.

"But I wasn't a child," I say. "Much worse has happened to others.

Who am I to take up your time when you could be helping the deserving cases?"

"Why does your story matter less?" she asks. Then all the fragments of a broken mirror start to fly out of my mind, and I see even more. That time when I was 16 and the man was 47 - it wasn't right. The time when I was 4 and the gang of boys were 10 - it wasn't right. *And then all the millions of mirror-dust microaggressions I used to just brush off, start to fall into my lap...*

One upon another, the secrets I've been keeping are fighting to get out. And not only that, they are fighting to be heard ... and seen ... and told out loud. They are fighting to use the right word. *It was rape*, they say. I still can't say that word without shrinking inside. I feel sick.

So, I know about the secret-keepers. I know why women don't speak out, keep small, stay invisible. There is safety in silence. At least, that's how it seems.

All my life, I've been fascinated by people. I could people-watch all day. The voice inside my head says, *but why? Why do they do that? Why do they say that, look like that, behave that way?* I guess that's what makes me a really good actress. Body language expert, Janine Driver, says that children who have experienced trauma or abuse become hypervigilant – and really good at reading people. Well, there we have it.

I do, in fact, count myself as an observer. I like to people watch, take my time and size things up before I join in. Even then I'm a listener, a quizzer, a great deflector - I can spend a whole conversation talking about you, revealing little about myself.

You see, in spite of being a performer and loving centre stage, I'm also good at hiding, blending in, ghosting.

The reason I became an actress was to hide. Hide behind characters and other personas. Hide behind a script, costumes and bright lights. Relate with a camera, emote with an inanimate object. Play to an audience I can't see. Be directed by someone else, just out of sight.

And all of it blissfully *not me*.

Hiding. Playing small. Concealing our feelings, our thoughts, ourselves. It's in our DNA.

Could it be down to what I refer to as our *Centuries of Pain*? The hundreds of years of being denied and existing only in relation to a man; as a daughter, wife, mother. We could be cast aside, accused of witchery, married off, banished, beheaded and battered - with church, community and government approval. And, in the ultimate gaslighting of all time, any woman becoming pregnant was not only the *only one responsible*, but also the one who would be punished. No wonder we needed to hide.

And here I am, living in a post-conflict society. A society where keeping silent was the safe option; secrecy was vital, a life and death decision. Even now, the post-conflict generation feel that keenly, and often subconsciously. It's been passed down in their DNA, the inter-generational trauma that keeps us repeating history.

Silence is safety. Secrets are sanctuary.

And yet. Keeping secrets often keeps the abuser safe, not us. Hiding, whilst understandable, can be at least as dangerous as speaking up.

Still.

We go on going on, because often we don't even recognise we have a choice.

I didn't report either of my rapes. I never spoke about them. I tucked them away inside for over 30 years. When I think about it, I didn't actually have the words to describe what happened, which seems extraordinary, considering how much I love language. I simply assumed I had somehow invited this violence and therefore the shame, and the secret, was mine to keep.

I grieve for that young woman. And with the lens of hindsight, age and wisdom, now see some of the choices that followed in a different light. No wonder. It sounds dramatic to say those incidents blighted my life, but they did, and in ways I still can't process. After university I had a breakdown, during which I spent three months plotting my own death, berating myself for not even being able to get that right. Then, one day when I was visiting my dad in North Yorkshire, I couldn't stop crying. He took one look and said, "Right, go back and pack up your stuff. You're going to come and work with me for the summer while you get your head straight." He owned a livery yard and I loved horses, so it became my healing process. Physical labour, routines, being outdoors, spending time with animals, it all soothed my scrambled brain and calmed my anxious body. He was wiser than he knew, my dad.

It felt like the depression had been with me from a young age, but I was finally diagnosed and treated in my mid-twenties. At the time I thought I was going mad, but now I know that depression is like a coldsore; always there, waiting to pop up when you haven't taken care of yourself. It never completely goes away, but if you get to know it better, it will serve as your personal alarm system. But in those early days it was terrifying.

I'd always loved drama at school, and it was my dad who suggested joining the local amateur dramatics society, with a view to meeting new people with a shared interest. For the next ten years, while I went travelling, met my first husband, bought a house and got on with life, I kept up the am dram productions, harbouring a secret ambition to become professional one day.

Which I finally did … studying at East15 Acting School and completing my MA in Acting for Media in 2004.

Fast forward to 2018, and I'm taking part in one of the most joyous productions of my life; I'm cast in the Vagina Monologues. We are an all-female cast with a female Director, Stage Manager and crew. It's hard to put into words how intoxicating that time was, how the rehearsal room fairly crackled with creativity and magic. How I skipped to work every morning, and at night, I couldn't wait to go to sleep so I could do it all again tomorrow. We raised money for Women's Aid; enough so that they could set up Northern Ireland's first rape-crisis line. It was right at the time of the Ulster Rugby Rape Trial and debates were taking place everywhere. It was all meant to be.

Women were finally talking; and it was all #metoo and #timesup and #ibelieveher

And yet.

We're still fighting, for equal pay, for improved legal services to facilitate rape trials, for better policing, for fairness and equality.

We are resilient as fuck. We are unstoppable.

And now I've turned all this resilience and experience into my own business as a Visibility Coach, empowering women to speak up, stand out and take courage from our sisters. We stand on the shoulders of the women before us and it's time to share our wisdom with the world. I love nothing more than running my *Speak with Confidence* workshops and watching women transform before my very eyes.

Take Katie who stood up to speak in front of the room – which she told me would have been unthinkable just two hours before. I suggested she stand with her feet a little wider apart, to help her feel anchored and grounded. She did and we all saw the immediate transformation. Katie couldn't believe it. "But I've been told to keep my legs together all my life. I tell my daughters to sit nicely and not take up room. Do you mean I can take up as much room as I like?" It always amazes me how something so small can make such a huge difference.

Or my 1:1 client Sarah, who had lost the ability to dream altogether. When I asked her what her goals were, she was literally lost for words. She couldn't articulate her dreams because she had spent a lifetime squashing her needs down in order to serve others. (Within a month she had not only articulated her dreams and goals, but had doubled her income and been promoted, hitting two of her goals in just two days).

Then there was Liz, doing such incredibly important work to keep our children safe online, who felt that posting on social media three times a week was intrusive and repetitive, sure she would be boring her audience. The thought of telling people the price of her consultations, brought her out in a cold sweat.

I get it.

Especially if you are an entrepreneur, where you have to be your business, and, essentially, sell yourself. It feels wrong and uncomfortable to talk about yourself, your skills, your wonderful wisdom and knowledge, even when you know 100% that you can help people. Despite my background, I found this aspect of running my own business super-squirmy.

For sure, acting has given me a way in; I've found some shortcuts. For example, I love, love, love talking to a camera. I know how to connect with my most anchored, truest voice. I can craft a good story. And I have approximately 2497 ways of getting over stage fright.

I also know the power of having someone in your corner, backing you up, putting you back together when you're feeling fragile. Guiding you without interfering in your creative process, supporting your choices while challenging your limiting beliefs. Like an A-list director, seeing the bigger picture when you can't.

Or, like a really great coach.

That's my superpower. And my happy place.

And when you get women together in a room (virtual or otherwise), you can easily 10x that power. We can combine our forces and create magic!

It's time to banish the overwhelm, rewrite the script and dazzle your way to a standing ovation - and an income you deserve. Because wealthy women will change the world and we need you now more than ever!

My Top Tips to Get More Visible (without beating yourself up about it)

Recognise your Visibility Blocks

Firstly, acknowledge that being visible is hard at times. Just like we're not always confident in every situation, being visible can feel daunting in certain spaces.

That said, being more visible and speaking up are skills that can be learned. None of us are born natural orators or feeling comfortable in the spotlight. But we can learn.

Become an observer of your own habits. Listen to your inner critic (but don't take those words on board) and be curious. The more you do this, the more natural it will become and you will soon start to notice patterns of behaviour.

If you're an avoider (hello fellow procrastinators and perfectionists!), note what your favourite avoidance tactic is and have a word with yourself next time you do it. For example, I was putting together a presentation and halfway through decided I needed a word cloud. I spent the next 45 minutes searching and creating word clouds online before I had a word with myself and said, *Hang on! This is my brain distracting me because it's a big job and I didn't take a break. Nobody needs a word cloud because nobody cares! Stop it! Get a cup of tea and get on with it.*

Push yourself out of your comfort zone. Find small ways that feel challenging to start with. If you feel like making videos is a huge mountain to climb, start with hitting *Record* every day. Narrate your walk to work or describe your surroundings. The content doesn't matter, what matters is you have taken the first tiny step, and after a week or two, hitting *Record* on your phone (and listening back to your voice) becomes the most natural thing in the world. Then move on to the next tiny step and so on.

Move – Breathe – Observe - Rest

Time to get out of your head. Just like I did after my breakdown, get outside and into nature. Connect with animals if you can. Do something physical; walk, dance, move. Sometimes even just getting out of your chair and standing up can change your energetic state, getting you out of overthinking and overwhelm. Meditate if that suits you. Definitely learn some breathing techniques to calm your nervous system. Become an observer of your thoughts, not an active participant. Take a rest. Amazing things happen when you rest your body. I was bedridden for a week once and had the most astonishingly creative ideas during that time.

Flip it

I often ask my clients to 'flip it' when they come up against resistance. Take Liz and her reluctance to charge for her services. When I asked her how she felt when other people asked to be paid for their services, she said "but of course! I wouldn't expect them to do it for free!" "So, what makes you so different?" I asked. This was a revelation to her, and we used the 'flip it' method several times during our time together. For example, when Liz felt she was being repetitive, I asked how she felt about seeing posts from the people she followed.

When you worry what people will think about you, flip it! If you're self-conscious about your voice or appearing on a screen, how do you feel when you see and hear others? Chances are you don't give it a second thought.

Follow Your Leader

I'm being flippant. I don't mean your leader per se, but follow the people you like and admire. Follow your competitors. There will always be someone ahead of you and someone behind you, in terms of experience and success in business, so model yourself on your business hero. Take a leaf out of their book and observe how they do things. Borrow a bit of their confidence, throw on your visibility cloak and give it a go. Think; *what would they do in this situation?* (When I was young we would always say "What would Madonna do?" whenever we felt unsure). You never know what might happen!

Your message is bigger than you

Finally, remember how important your message is. You could say what my friend Holly-Ann says, whenever she gets nervous or wants to avoid making her (brilliant) marketing videos, which is "my message is bigger than me". It is! If we don't tell our stories, and thus market our businesses or connect with our audience, no-one will ever know how we can help them or what solutions we offer to their problems. And maybe, just maybe, you will find that telling your story will offer someone the opportunity to share theirs too. *That* ripple effect is truly unstoppable.

VICKY BLADES

Vicky is a professional actress, aspiring writer and unstoppable Communications Coach! She has a mission to show women how to speak up and be heard by finding their authentic voice and developing the confidence to step powerfully into the spotlight and take centre stage; at work, in life, and in business.

She knows the hiding habits of women too well; after all, she became an actress to hide behind characters and scripts, costumes and screens. She also kept a life-changing event secret for 30 years and is still working through the repercussions of that, and the consequences of not speaking up.

Finding out why women find it hard to play big has led Vicky to discover that, all too often, women are the secret-keepers. But to what cost? It's time to challenge this narrative and stop our collective suffering in silence! She knows your message is important and it's time to get it out into the world. She also knows how difficult that can feel. But in gathering women together and telling our stories, we create magic, and that makes us all Unstoppable!

Vicky's LinkedIn is www.linkedin.com/in/vickyblades

WHAT IF?
CARA QUINN

2017. The year I turned forty. The worst year of my life. The turning point.

This was the year I realised my big plan for life was never going to happen. And when I say, *big plan,* I really mean *a standard, everyday sort of plan.* The sort of plan that everyone around me seemed to have no bother fulfilling. You see, all I had ever wanted in life, my only goal or vision, was to find a nice man, get married and have kids. Not exactly the most ambitious dream, but it was all I believed life was about. Without it, what was the point?

So, when I found myself in my fortieth year, having achieved precisely none of those things, its fair to say I was NOT in a good place. Newly single and recently diagnosed with the 'cancer gene', I had no man and, soon to be, no womb. It was game over for my one and only dream.

And so ensued months of heartbreak and grieving for the life I would never have. Living alone in my cold, damp-ridden house – I wallowed. I was a failure at life and an embarrassment to myself. I spent the year under a thick fog, going through the motions of life, working all week and partying hard at the weekend.

Ahh, the weekend! The time to escape the reality of my shitshow life and drown my sorrows in copious amounts of alcohol. That'll do the trick! And it did … well … at least it did for the first few drinks. Of course, stopping after a few drinks was never my forte, so with no 'off button', I sped through the stages of 'merry drunk', 'affectionate drunk' and 'overconfident drunk', before crash-landing in 'depressive drunk' and finally calling it a night at 'pass out drunk'.

When Depressive Drunk Cara showed up, it was never pretty. She thrived on welcoming all the deep, dark, murky thoughts out to play. Like clockwork, I would end up inconsolable, crying into my vodka and calling myself all the pathetic losers of the day, much to the dismay of my ever-patient family and friends. But I would not be told different. I knew best. I was worthless.

Hangover days weren't much craic either. An abundance of all the same thoughts flowed, topped off with a healthy measure of 'hanxiety' and a nice dollop of shame. Something had to give … and thankfully, it did.

ENTER INTO MY LIFE – SELF-REFLECTION

After accidentally downloading a book which I thought was about all things mystical and otherworldly, I was disappointed to realise that this was a book I actually had to participate in. This book required me to go on a journey of self-reflection. Yikes! Never being one to not finish a book I had started, I grabbed my notebook and pen and ploughed on regardless.

In one weekend, I read that book cover to cover, and my life changed forever.

Suddenly the blinders were removed, and I could see all the negative patterns I had been repeating, the thoughts they had sprung from and the deep-rooted beliefs that gave them life. The soul-destroying assertions that I was *not good enough*, *not lovable* and *not worthy* were all decided by a naive little girl who didn't know better and had been allowed to take the reins of my life for far too long. But no more. It was my turn now.

Over the months that followed, with a new sense of purpose and joy that I'd never before experienced, I learnt all I could about the power of the mind. Courses, books, audiobooks, podcasts, videos – if the content was inspiring, motivating and transformational, I had to have it in my life. With clarity and determination, I went about dismantling all those old, negative mental constructs I had created and, brick by brick, the walls came down. In its place, my self-belief was sparked and each day it started to burn brighter.

Gradually, with this new-found peace of mind and fresh outlook, I started to make different choices and my life began to change. I began to care about my surroundings and put some love back into the house I once hated. I realised I actually had a lot to be grateful for. I started to dream about what a new home would be like and challenged the negative whispers in my mind of *it's never going to be possible* and *it's far too risky*. I decided I was ready to take that risk! And once I did, everything fell into place. I found a new-build site I adored, and with the race on to secure it, I managed to agree sale on my own house within just twenty-four hours. Five months later, I had moved into a beautiful home and a neighbourhood that I loved.

I stopped wasting my days and found new things to fill it. I tore myself away from Netflix, got up off the sofa and out of my comfort zone. I started to do things I would never have considered before … ON MY OWN! I attended events, I took up yoga, I started taking walks and I got healthy. I explored all sorts of holistic approaches to healing and went on a mission to clear out the old and welcome in the new. And the results showed.

During COVID, when walks were all the rage, I was out at the park with a friend. We bumped into a lady who had her gorgeous little dog with her, and a seed was sown in my mind. I looked at that furry wee pooch and its cheery disposition and I thought, *I could see myself with a dog like that one day.* Never having been much of an animal lover before, this was an unusual thought for me. My sister had often tried to talk me into getting a pup, but I always insisted 'I'm no good with dogs', 'dogs can sense my fear', 'I couldn't manage a dog', 'absolutely NO'!

Something had shifted though. I kept thinking about that brief encounter at the park. My usual thoughts of *no, what do I know about dogs?* and *a dog would wreck my beautiful new house* went through my mind, but now they were accompanied by a quieter little voice saying, *what if?* Oddly, over the next few days, dogs started to come up in conversation and a couple of people asked me if it was ever something I'd consider. Even stranger, I found myself not saying the usual 'no no no'. Instead, I heard myself say things like, 'It's something I'm toying with ... maybe one day ...'

From then on, the idea built momentum and I started to question all the stories I was telling myself about why I should never have a dog. *Were they really true? Was there another possibility that I hadn't considered? Maybe there was a way I could find a dog breed that was small and known for their softer temperament – something even I could handle. Maybe I could learn how to train a dog. Maybe it wouldn't hurt to just have a look ...*

So, I discovered the breed of the dog I had met that day, and I started my search. Before I knew it, I was 'all in'. I had bought a crate, toys, bowls and a collar, all in anticipation of my new furry friend. Eventually, after constant searches on all the sites, I refreshed a webpage and a new litter of cavachons appeared. Two weeks later, I met crazy little Coco and fell in love.

Serendipitously, when I got Coco home later that day, I opened her paperwork and noticed the date she was born ... the very same date, two months previous, when I took a walk in the park with a friend. Magic.

So, life was good. I was different. I was happy. But, as I settled into this new way of being, something started to stir within me. There had to be something more. What did I want to get out of my life? I had absolutely no idea. My first forty years were all taken up with the notion that I had to have the perfect nuclear family, but now there was space for something else. In all my time, I had never really stopped to consider what my own ambitions were. I had no hobbies, interests or passions. I had never done anything extracurricular other than hang out with friends and family or watch TV. So, what did I want out of life?

I reflected on the little girl at school, terrified of speaking up, of saying the wrong thing and whose face went crimson if the teacher asked her a question. I saw how she carried those same traits through her teenage years and then to university. Always scared to say what she thought, keeping a low profile in lectures, doing enough to get by, but never really believing she was capable of much. I observed how she drifted into a career in recruitment, yet despite being all grown up, nothing had really changed – she was still hiding and playing small.

Although she slowly moved through the ranks in her career, I watched as she compared herself to those around her and stressed at the thought of anyone realising how incapable she really was. In meetings with her seniors, it was like being back in the classroom. She prayed the attention would never land on her. With heart palpitations and sweaty palms, she would sit, eyes down, dreading that *today* would be the day she was finally exposed as the fraud she was. She knew with certainty she was, quite simply, not the same calibre as those around her, and it was only a matter of time before everyone else knew it too.

Ah, Cara, if only you had actually known the truth. What path would you have taken? What could you have achieved? What heights could you have reached?

I thought about my current role, and while I enjoyed working in a feel-good discipline that gave people jobs, it was never something I had proactively set out to be part of. I pondered my skills and considered what I was really capable of. *If I wasn't doing this, what could I be doing? When were the times in my career I really felt alive?*

And then it hit me. I loved seeing and helping people succeed. I also thought of the times I had interviewed amazingly talented people who missed out on opportunities that could have been theirs for the taking. I recognised that many were just like I had been – lacking in confidence and riddled with imposter syndrome. I thought of how they showed up at an interview with no self-belief and so, unsurprisingly, failed to convince anyone else to believe in them either.

As I mulled it all over, I considered how my own journey to empowering myself was the missing key. If I could share what I had learnt from shifting my own mindset, and combine it with my understanding of career progression and recruiting, surely, I could give people the tools they needed to get out of their own way, find their passions and go for their dreams. Maybe I could even make a business out of it. And so, the idea was born.

True to form though, it didn't take long for the negative chatter to chime in with its perspective: *Wise up, Cara! Get a grip! What do you know about running a business? What if you fail? What if you lose your house? You're perfectly fine as you are.* By this time though, I was getting pretty well-practised at dealing with my wayward mind and flipping those thoughts into something more positive. I changed tack. *What if it actually worked? What if I spent my days doing something I truly loved? What if I could help people believe in themselves too? Oh, I wonder …*

And so, the notion of having my own business started to take shape. It was baby steps at first; simply getting used to it in my own head. Then I eventually vocalised it and shared my idea with someone. Then another person and another. Next, I was formalising my knowledge and getting qualifications in NLP (neurolinguistic programming) and coaching. Before I knew it, I was brainstorming business names and buying a domain.

Finally, the time came where I would have to take a leap of faith. I knew what I wanted, but there was no denying it – it was terrifying. After much reflection and looking at it from all angles, I resolved that trying and failing was something I could live with much easier than if I gave up on myself and my dream. That's when it all clicked into place and I knew with certainty what had to be done. I took a deep breath, summoned all my courage, handed in my notice and created Stellar Impact.

Today, I'm loving life and can't imagine doing anything else. The joy I get from seeing my clients learn to trust in themselves and succeed is incomparable. Although growing a business hasn't always been easy, it's a challenge I am 100% up for. When my mind starts wrecking the peace, as it often still does, I am wise to it. I am more resilient than I've ever been and I have a toolkit of tried and tested ways to take back control and find my inner calm.

So, if you find yourself stuck in a rut, believing you can't go for your dreams, if you talk to yourself like you wouldn't talk to your worst enemy, if you believe you aren't capable or deserving of getting what you want from life, then now is the time to STOP and take note.

The first step in making a change is to pay attention to the thoughts that run riot in your mind. It's time to reflect, get honest and ask yourself – *Are these stories even true?* Are they 100% fact, or are they simply unchallenged beliefs you have held about yourself? When these misconceptions are revealed for what they really are, they lose their grip on you. You no longer have to accept this demoralising self-talk as fact. Better still, you can create a new narrative that will remind you of how amazing you are and what you have to offer the world. You are capable of whatever you put your mind to.

Ask yourself: *Where would I be without these thoughts? What if I knew, with 100% certainty, that I couldn't fail? What could I do? Who would I be? What could I achieve?*

Allow yourself to dream ...

I did.

CARA QUINN

C ara Quinn is a passionate and skilled career and mindset coach, certified NLP (neurolinguistic programming) practitioner and the founder of Stellar Impact. Her aim is to empower people with the confidence, skills and strategies to conquer their fears and doubts, pursue their dreams and reach their true potential.

After achieving an MA (Hons) at the University of Dundee, Cara subsequently completed a graduate management program which led her to specialise in the HR field of recruitment. Since then, she has accrued an impressive track record spanning over two decades in the corporate recruiting world. During this time, she also attained a postgrad diploma in personnel and development from Queen's University Belfast.

Throughout her career in talent acquisition, Cara witnessed first-hand the profound impact that negative thinking, low confidence and imposter syndrome can have on an individual's career trajectory. All too often she saw talented individuals miss out on opportunities because they lacked the self-belief to go for what they want or sell themselves effectively. Having overcome these challenges herself, she became passionate about helping others do the same.

Through Stellar Impact, Cara brings a unique blend of personal experience and professional expertise to help her clients navigate their thought patterns and excel in their careers. Offering a range of transformative workshops and coaching services, she equips people with the practical knowledge and tools to overcome obstacles, create a positive mindset, cultivate confidence and achieve unstoppable success.

Cara's LinkedIn is www.linkedin.com/in/cara-quinn-coach

HOW DECLUTTERING CAN CHANGE YOUR LIFE
SHARON McNULTY

"It's not about the stuff - it's the effect the stuff has on our life"

Consider the last time you were searching for something; it may have been several weeks ago, several days ago or as recent as this morning. How did you feel when searching? Anecdotal evidence would suggest that you may have felt frustrated, irritated, annoyed or even angry.

By the time, we are 70 years old, we will have spent an average of 355 days searching for items. That's almost one year of our lives spent frustrated, irritated, annoyed and angry. That can't be good for our well-being. However, the good news is, it is something we can change.

Creating an organised and serene environment, not only reduces our stress but also contributes to better mental health and overall well-being. However, the journey to declutter is more than creating a tidy space, it becomes a gateway to unlocking a life of unstoppable potential.

MY STORY

I am director of the business, *Joyful Spaces;* an award winning, internationally renowned professional organiser, with clients around the world. I have 9 years' experience working one to one with clients, organising and transforming their space and ultimately transforming their lives. I live my definition of order; my home and office have the most beautiful energy. They are neat, orderly and easy to keep tidy.

However, it wasn't always this way. Let me take you back to 2010, when I was a single mother of three, struggling to balance work and parenting, as well as keep a tidy home. Despite my attempts to stay organised, the sheer volume of possessions overwhelmed me.

The never-ending paperwork became an immense burden. I held onto every single piece, including payslips from as far back as 1989, without being able to distinguish what was truly important. The frustration grew as I constantly searched for items, knowing they were filed somewhere in the vast sea of documents. The sheer volume became overwhelming.

I was an expert in tidying as I spent so much time on it - or so I thought! In hindsight, I realise that what I considered expertise was, in fact, a cycle of inefficiency and wasted time. I had too much stuff and didn't know how to let go of the items I didn't love or need. This insight became a turning point, leading me to re-evaluate my approach to *tidying*.

I came upon Marie Kondo's book on organising my home and put it into practice. It transformed my home, my office and my life. My overwhelm was replaced with order, calm and joy. I decided I wanted to help others in the same situation, so I trained under Marie Kondo as a consultant and, thanks to the referrals I received from my wonderful clients, I have now reached the highest level possible, as a Master certified Consultant, the equivalent to having a black belt in tidying.

I decided to find out as much as I could about clutter and completed extensive research into it. I realised that the challenges of mess and disorder extend beyond homeowners to businesses, who often underestimate the impact it has on their operations. This realisation led me to embark on a mission to assist businesses in organising, optimising and transforming their spaces for improved efficiency and productivity.

Once clients experienced the transformative power of tidying and organising, they gained clarity, concentration and productivity. I helped so many people to do this, that I was asked to co-author a number-one best-selling book because of my successful methods.

WHY DOES CLUTTER AFFECT US?

Everything around us is in a constant state of vibration; the chair, desk, the tree. Nothing is ever static. Everything is energy, perpetually moving or vibrating. Every object, person and living being is constantly in motion, vibrating at a specific frequency. Just because we can't see the energy transmission, doesn't mean it isn't happening.

When we enter a cluttered room, the energy in that room is stagnant and there's a shift in our body both physically and emotionally; it induces a sense of lethargy, with little motivation and we adopt a pessimistic mindset. Our vibrations and energies are low. This stagnant energy disempowers us, it creates inertia, causes procrastination and prevents us from living life to its fullest potential.

When we avoid dealing with physical clutter, we avoid dealing with it emotionally, causing this energy to become entrenched and stagnant. Tackling the mess can be overwhelming, physically and mentally, and there are items in our homes that we do not love but feel obliged to keep.

Many of our items hold an emotional attachment for us, both positive and negative, and parting with them requires processing these emotions. Often, it seems easier to hold onto the item than deal with the emotions attached to it. The fear that *we might need it someday* perpetuates this cycle, despite the likelihood that such a day rarely arrives. Another reason we hold onto these items is the belief that we have *spent our hard-earned money to buy them*. We feel it would be wasteful to let these items go. It is crucial to recognise that keeping items we don't love, use or need is the true waste, especially when someone else would find joy in owning them.

The impact of decluttering goes beyond our personal space, it transforms every aspect of our lives. Letting go of what doesn't serve us, whether it's physical clutter, toxic relationships or negative thoughts, creates space for items we love, which in turn, raises our vibrations and attracts more positivity into our life. After witnessing the transformation in my own life, I was inspired to share this system with others. Let me illustrate the universal power of decluttering and share the story of three remarkable clients who, like me, embarked on a journey to reshape their environment and in turn their lives.

EMILY

The power of decluttering is transformative, it is the catalyst for huge change, and this was evident with my client, Emily, a mental health advocate and mum of 3. Emily reached out to me to help declutter her home. As Emily and I began working together, little did we know the incredible journey awaiting her. As we cleared the area under her stairs, we converted it into a cosy nook, placing a table, chair and book case there. We had unintentionally created a secluded haven in the heart of her home, a space that radiated positive energy. This marked the beginning of her unstoppable journey.

Decluttering her home and shaping this cosy nook gave Emily the mental and physical haven to write; it became the space where she wrote her first book. Emily was always aware that she possessed a story worth telling, yet the idea of becoming an author never dawned on her. However, as she sat in this space, she felt compelled to pen her story.

From that moment on, Emily's life transformed as she authored three best-selling books, left her 22-year career, and started her own business dedicated to doing what she loves and making a meaningful difference for others. Emily's journey exemplifies the essence of being unstoppable, and I firmly believe she is just getting started.

JOAN

Joan was a client who always kept a tidy house until she moved home to care for her sick father. Bringing the contents of her flat to her childhood home, she stored them in the spare room. Her belongings soon accumulated and spread throughout the house, turning every room into a chaotic and disorganised space.

This disorganisation started to affect Joan's mental health and well-being. She became anxious at the state of disarray and she found herself avoiding the cluttered rooms; she dreaded opening the door. Going through these items was too overwhelming and she (wrongly) believed she was lazy, comparing herself with others who kept a tidy home.

This began to have a huge negative impact on every part of her life, especially her mental health. She didn't ask visitors into her home as she was too embarrassed, and instead met her partner in a local hotel. She withdrew from social interactions, and wondered if life was worth living.

However, when Joan reached out for support and we started the decluttering process, she began to regain control. For the first time in a while, she saw joy in her belongings and glimpsed a brighter future. Fast forward to today, as Joan eagerly awaits the arrival of her first baby, and the positive changes in her life have not only given her renewed hope and purpose but have also made her feel truly unstoppable in the face of adversity.

CARLA

My client Carla's remarkable journey embodies the essence of being unstoppable. She was stuck in her life, her mind was full of so many things she had to do, that it took 2 A4 pages to write them down. One of these pressing matters was getting her home in order. Overwhelmed by the sheer magnitude of it all, she reached out to me for support.

During our conversation, I tried to explain to Carla how freeing it would feel once she had decluttered her living space, how everything would finally have a place and how her home would be easy to keep tidy. However, amidst the chaos and overwhelm, Carla found it hard to see how this would be possible.

I told her to borrow my belief—which she did. Carla knew she didn't want to stay in the same place so, while she felt a glimmer of scepticism, she decided to embrace the process.

The transformation that occurred was nothing short of amazing. Carla felt clarity for the first time in a long time. By letting go of all the stuff that was weighing her down, she had the capacity to think. She became confident in making decisions, as she made so many decisions on what to keep and what to let go of through this process.

The decluttering process allowed her to understand what she loved and what she didn't love, and she came to the realisation that she didn't love her job. After 36 years in one profession, she decided on a career change, so she undertook further training and set up her own business doing what she loved. Within a short space of time, business was going so well she left her full-time job.

Shortly after this, Carla could see so much potential in her home that she decided to renovate it. She has created the most stunning home for herself and her two boys, and Carla attributed these monumental life changes to the simple act of decluttering her home. Taking that first step of tackling her living space allowed her to believe that anything was possible.

MY TAKEAWAYS

Living in a cluttered and disorganised home can take a toll on your emotional well-being. It can leave you feeling overwhelmed, anxious and drained. It is my firm belief that everyone deserves a well-organised, inspiring and joyful workspace. No matter where you are starting from or how messy you feel your space feels, with my proven system, we can reshape your environment and unlock your full potential for success.

Studies have shown that the space we live and work in significantly impacts our mood, productivity and mental wellbeing. It's hard to feel relaxed in a messy home!

Look at your present environment and consider how you feel. Do you feel relaxed and at ease or, are you feeling unsettled and anxious? If it is the latter, and you are feeling dissatisfied with your current environment, that is good because you will be inspired to create something better.

Most of us have too much stuff and we just don't know where to start. Our sense of overwhelm leads to procrastination and inertia. When we finally start, we often approach it by tidying room by room or cupboard by cupboard, but what we're doing is moving our stuff from one place to another, and this is ineffective. You can superficially tidy in a short time, yet it will return to its previous state very quickly. If you declutter half-heartedly, you will get half-hearted results, and this increases the possibility of rebound.

If you have been tidying this way for years, your results will show how effective that is. So, how about trying something different? Something that will help you fall in love with your home again. To transform your space, create a haven of calmness and serenity, and unlock your unstoppable potential, consider these takeaways:

1. Commit to tidying up – put a date in your diary to do so each week and stick to this time.

2. Take 20 minutes and sit in your favourite part of your home. Think about your ideal home, consider what you would like your home to look like and how you want to feel in your home. Write this down and on those days, you can't be bothered to tidy, look at this and you will feel motivated again.

3. Start by organising one drawer, one cupboard or one corner. This will show quick progress and get the momentum going.

4. Gather similar items together, for example, gather your coats from around your home and bring them together. This is important preparation and will streamline your tidying journey.

5. It is only when you do organise similar items together that you will know how many of each item you own and you can come to the realisation that you have enough, you won't go without.

6. Choose only those items you love or need – ask yourself if you are

excited to wear or use it? Do you feel amazing wearing it? if you struggle with this, ask yourself if you would you spend the time, energy, and money on getting it repaired.

7. Let the rest go with love, with gratitude. Many people hold onto items, because letting them go would be wasteful, however, remember it is wasteful to have something and not need it or use it, especially when someone else would love to have it. Don't offer it to your friend/sister/mother unless you know they would buy it at full price in a shop.

8. Display only those items you are currently using and set up a "home shop" to store the excess. Set up the shop like a supermarket shelf, with similar items grouped together and place those needing used first at the front. Once you need to replenish an item, check if it "is in stock" in your shop before you buy. This will save you so much money.

9. Note: The "shop" is usually in a spare cupboard found during your decluttering journey. As you use up the excess items, these areas become available, making your home organised and efficient.

10. Give everything a place, and when you are finished using it, return it there.

11. Every evening before bedtime, reset your home. Fold up the throws and plump up the pillows. This only takes 5-10 minutes and means every morning when you come down, your home will look beautiful.

In the pursuit of a serene, organised space, we have explored the profound impact that decluttering has had on both personal and client experiences. From the frustration of endless searching to the transformative stories of Emily, Joan and Carla, it is evident that decluttering is a catalyst for monumental change. We unlock more than just a physical space; we open a gateway to mental clarity, purpose and an unstoppable potential that lies within each of us.

SHARON MCNULTY

Sharon McNulty, from Joyful Spaces is a multi-award winning, internationally renowned professional organiser, with clients around the world. She has 9 years' experience working 1:1 with clients organising and transforming their homes and businesses and ultimately transforming their lives.

And, thanks to the referrals she received from her clients, she has now reached the highest level possible as a Master certified Consultant (which is akin to having a black belt in tidying and organising). Sharon lives her definition of order; her home has the most beautiful energy. It is neat, orderly, and so easy to keep tidy.

However, Sharon's journey to here hasn't always been smooth. In 2014, as a single mother of three, she struggled to balance work, childcare, and maintaining a tidy home. No matter how hard she tried, she couldn't keep on top of it. She was quite organised, but just had too much stuff, Sharon was overwhelmed and didn't know where to start, she was going round in circles, spending precious time moving this stuff around- in her mind she was tidying it!

Sharon came upon Marie Kondo's book on organising her home and put it into practice. It transformed her home and her life. Her overwhelm was replaced with order, calm and joy. And she decided she wanted to help others in the same situation, so she trained under Marie Kondo as a consultant.

And she decided to find out as much as she could about clutter and completed extensive research on it and from that, co-authored a number 1 best-selling book, where she explored how our messy homes affect us physically, mentally, and financially.

Sharon realised that the challenges of mess and disorder extend beyond homeowners to businesses, who often underestimate the impact it has on their operations. This realisation led her to embark on a mission to assist businesses in organising, optimising, and transforming their spaces for improved efficiency and productivity.

Sharon believes that everyone deserves an organised, inspiring, and joyful workspace that unlocks their full potential for success. It is her mission to empower businesses to create such workspaces, one business at a time.

Sharon's website is www.joyfulspaces.co.uk

BROKEN OPEN
BRIANA McATEER

"We have two lives, and the second begins when we realize we only have one." – Confucius
"I believe we have two lives. The life we learn with and the life we live with after that." – Iris Gaines

At eight years old I made a pledge to myself. I pledged I wouldn't live my life held hostage by invisible barriers and conditioning that seemed to be dictating the lives of the adults I saw. It seemed to fuel their rage, thwarted their success and stopped them from living a life they loved. To me, being unstoppable doesn't mean achieving lots of external accolades, but having the consciousness in any moment to be able to respond rather than react. It's about having the freedom of will to create an intentional life rather than reproduce a life on autopilot. I would come to learn this requires you to shed versions of yourself that feel safer maintaining the status-quo and layers of conditioning that keep you repeating cycles. It's not so much about *becoming* unstoppable, but deepening your connection with yourself, so you can *remember* that you already are. It happens when everything is frustratingly unclear; when the ground beneath you feels like it's collapsing and you feel the least like yourself… this is where you begin to cultivate the characteristic of "unstoppable." If you're living this kind of unstoppable life, it'll feel like you've lived four or five different lives as you get called through several initiations.

This particular chapter of my story starts with my first real initiation, or what I call, my broken-open moment.

I woke up that morning the same as every morning for the last few months: on a mattress on the floor of my sister's one-bedroom apartment with a disconcerting empty feeling. I felt like a shell of a person with nothing inside. This was quickly replaced with immense grief and sadness that had me sobbing almost immediately after waking.

Throughout the days, for six months, I would oscillate between an uncomfortably numb feeling and overwhelming sadness. The sobbing started the moment I woke up and basically continued throughout the day. There was barely an inch of the city I hadn't been seen crying in. If I had asked someone, I'm sure they would have told me I was depressed, but I wasn't interested in a diagnosis. I knew the grief and sadness were completely appropriate for how much I had hated, abandoned and rejected myself in the years previous.

I was 24 and had spent most of my life living inside a head telling me I wasn't good enough – not pretty enough, not thin enough, not out-going enough, not easy-going enough, not fun enough, not interesting enough… and also… too angry, too intense, too needy, too smart, too much of a know-it-all, too bossy, too pushy – this list could go on for a while.

Chasing approval ran so deep in me I didn't even realise I was doing it. I became more outgoing by drinking and dancing on tables. I avoided rejection by never saying 'no'. I gained my approval by being a fun party girl. I spent a night in a meth den because somehow that meant I was easy-going. I ended up alone on a house boat with two much older men I didn't know that well, because I didn't want to appear difficult. I ended up doing drugs with some random dude in a bar in Amsterdam because of how "fun" I was. I stopped counting my sexual partners at 50. I'd only eat once a day (or not at all after a night of drug taking) so I could be skinny and finally feel good enough. Every interaction I had with food was a way of restricting, punishing, rejecting, abandoning, denying or hating myself. My body had gotten so thin and neglected that people were asking if I was doing OK.

For years I had deemed me, as I am, not worthy or good "enough". I took every opportunity to abandon or reject who I was or what I wanted, in favour of being who or what I thought would get people to like me. It had finally caught up with me. I was absolutely broken. I was so tired of hating myself. So tired of being at war with my body. So tired of trying so hard and getting nowhere. So tired of pretending. So tired of trying to be liked. So tired.

The question that filled my days was 'why was I so willing to abandon myself to please people who literally didn't give a shit about me?'

The answer? Trauma.

My people pleasing (fawn response), perfectionism, binge drinking, drug-taking, restrictive and controlling diets, promiscuity, chaotic and emotionally abusive romantic relationships, never feeling like I fit in, my complete system shut down when asked to speak in front of people, my inability to sustain relationships, my rage, my hypervigilance, my hyper-sense of responsibility, the way I flinched when anyone touched me…all responses to trauma, and the list goes on and on and on.

I struggled a bit with this because I didn't experience any "traumatic event". No near-death experiences. I was never raped or abused. I wasn't beaten or homeless or abandoned. For the first 12 years of my life, I lived with two parents I knew loved me. I was always provided for, I went to bed fed and warm every night. Neither of them had any substance abuse issues and in that time we didn't experience any financial hardship.

So why then would so much of my life have been taken over by trauma? What even is trauma?

I like Dr Valerie Rein's definition:

"Trauma is any experience that made you feel unsafe in your fullest authentic expression and led to developing trauma adaptations to keep you safe."

Trauma can fall into three categories; personal experience, generational and collective.

My personal experience of trauma, that are pertinent to this story, is my relationship with my mother and the trauma of emotional abuse. It's one thing to say, "I experienced childhood trauma," it's an entirely different thing to acknowledge, "I was abused by my mother." It's been difficult for me to get my head around it. Abuse seems like a strong word. When you hear 'abuse' you think of news stories about children locked in basements or being beaten. (I should say, while I was never beaten, I did witness this happening in my family). This is the same mother who tucked me in at night, who kissed my scraped knees, who spent hours of my life cradling and hugging me; the same woman who devoted so much of her energy to being a "good" mother. I had a relatively "normal" childhood. At least from the outside.

She was, at times, a nurturing mother but I often describe her as Jekyll and Hyde. She was also plagued with her own trauma and anxiety that she had to dispel somewhere. As a child I could never predict what was going to set her off. Going shopping for clothes always sticks out for me because invariably I would be left feeling cowed and embarrassed as she screamed at me in public for not wanting to try on the t-shirt she picked out for me. I was grabbed, had my hair pulled and was hit when I didn't comply, didn't react quick enough or didn't respond in a "respectable" way. I was screamed at, called names and shamed when *how I was* didn't suit her. I spent a lot of time on my own, either being isolated or eventually isolating myself. Even at 27 years old, she backed me into a corner goading me to punch her in the face. I don't' even remember what that was about. I often wondered why she couldn't see, or didn't care, how sad and worthless I felt when she was screaming at me.

The instability of this, the unpredictability of this, wreaked havoc on my system. It wasn't safe for me to be in my 'fullest authentic expression'. It wasn't safe for me to relax. I became hypervigilant. I had spent my life up until this point trying to outrun two emotions: worthlessness and rejection.

My relationship with my mother also represents the intergenerational trauma in my life. As a Catholic woman in Northern Ireland, the trauma of colonisation is passed down intergenerationally. The decades of The Troubles, witnessed and lived through by her, another trauma passed down. Women in Northern Ireland had to be guarded and defensive against many assaults – physically, emotionally, culturally and ideologically. My mother was typical in this way.

My mother, like all of our mothers, was a product of a patriarchal system. Living in a patriarchy permeates every area of a women's life. It dictates the relationship she has with her body, the relationship she has with her emotional life, the relationship she has with her desires, her sexuality, her ability to nourish herself, how she parents and shapes the relationship she has with herself. In every area, a woman learns her life is worth-less than a man's. She learns parts of her are problematic. She learns her worth is conditional. She learns that having desires isn't safe, to be in her body isn't safe, being overly emotional isn't safe. To be a woman in her *fullest authentic expression* isn't safe. She learns to cut herself off from her desires. She learns to reject her sexuality. She learns to shut down her emotions. She internalised the oppression and creates a shaming and harsh inner reality that does the job at keeping her small, insignificant and compliant.

My mother, like all of our mothers, like all of us are subject to these traumas. There were so many ways in which she had to abandon and reject herself. As an adult, who's now a mother, I can see her. I can see her without judgement. I can see her pain. I can see her struggle. I can see how hard she was fighting for her own survival. A woman who has lost touch with her ability to nurture herself, who is actively rejecting and shaming herself, cannot provide nurturing, unconditional acceptance and care for her daughter; a daughter who comes and triggers every one of those lost parts of her. Seeing it from this depth and with this clarity also makes my seemingly self-destructive behaviours make sense.

Women have been oppressed for millennia, oppression is traumatising, trauma is passed down through the generations. The collective and generational trauma of rejection and worthlessness imprinted on my mother became my personal, collective and generational experience of trauma.

I had been trying to outrun this unconscious sense of worthlessness by trying to meet the conditions of my worthiness. Trying to be thin enough, trying to be likable, trying not to be too difficult, being desirable without being too sexy etc. Meeting conditions of an oppressive culture is never going to end with a feeling of worthiness. Sticking to a diet was never going to address my willingness to completely abandon myself for the approval of others.

Trauma stops us in our tracks. We become stuck in a moment in time; reacting to the past instead of responding to the present. To become unstoppable, as I define it, first requires that we see this invisible matrix that has been making the decisions for us in our life. See how it has been taking away our freewill. It keeps us on a shame-based diet hamster-wheel; it keeps us tolerating behaviours in relationships or at work that damage our health; it keeps us in a people-pleasing, perfectionist performance.

Being unstoppable requires that we start living in our body again so that we can stop trying to out-run our emotions. I, like all the women I work with, had escaped up into my head; becoming rational and reasonable and detached from my emotional experience. Those six months on that mattress were my training ground for starting this work. It was an intensive period for getting to know myself; learning to meet those parts of myself I had abandoned. I got to practice sitting with emotions, sitting with the pain and discomfort. I began facing and accepting parts of myself I had long rejected.

My version of unstoppable requires that we excavate the ways we have *internalised* the shaming and oppressive culture. I was no longer being oppressed by a system or a person. I was doing an incredibly good job of that myself. Self-criticism and judgement became tools to keep myself "in-line." Of course we would internalise the oppression. Keeping ourselves small and cowed is how we maintain our sense of "safety". It also operates like a cage keeping us locked in realities that are not ours. Internalised oppression will not allow us to be unstoppable, it's too dangerous. When we can see this and start to view our reality from compassion and curiosity, we dissolve this cage and can begin to make deliberate decisions rather than fearful reactions.

Importantly, it requires that we move our nervous system out of a state of hypervigilance, working with the body to create a new sense of safety. Showing our body that it is actually safe to take up space; it is actually safe to speak up; it is actually safe to relax, play, desire, feel and nurture. When we can allow the nervous system to thaw into a softer reality, we begin to make decisions that enhance the felt experience of pleasure. Once we begin to taste this, we stop accepting less than what feels good.

My mom passed away before I was fully able to understand what was happening for me and before we were able to make any meaningful shift in the dynamic of our relationship. One year after my mom passed away, my first daughter was born. We named her Sarah after her grandma, my mother.

My beloved baby girl came in with the force, strength and resilience of her grandma. And she came requiring of me all the parts I hadn't yet developed. As I triggered parts of my mother, my daughter triggered parts of me I had still been abandoning.

One day when she was three years old, she was hitting me. As per the parenting books, I was holding her arms explaining 'I wasn't going to allow her to hit me.' So she bit me on the wrist. A second passed before I started crying. So much happened in that second. I was flooded with the rage of someone who'd been aggressed many times, immediately followed by the helplessness of someone who'd been overpowered many times. The tears were tears of years of suppression.

This moment called me into my next initiation. An initiation I'm still in as I write this. This one is calling me to truly step into the archetypal mother; matriarch. To hold the kind of space I want for my girls, and to shoulder some of the trauma for them. I am reclaiming my power and dignity that had been suffocated by my experience of trauma. I'm coming back to the steps I mentioned above to deepen my relationship with myself, step out of the cage trauma creates and make more *decisions* that bring me into deeper commune with my emotional life.

My girls will not experience the degree of rejection and abandonment and feel the worthlessness that the generations before them had to. For the trauma my mom passed down to me, she also passed down incredible strength, resilience, determination and a powerful love that makes the pain and discomfort of facing and moving through trauma an unquestionable and doable afterthought.

With each layer of trauma I shed, my life becomes lighter. I no longer view myself from the lens of *"what's wrong with me?"*, instead get to experience softness that comes from compassionate curiosity. I get to experience the other half of the emotional spectrum; genuine joy, ease and playfulness.

I get to look around at the life I've created and realise I *want* everything that I have. I have a marriage to a man to whom I connect deeper to every year. We're on this ride of discovery and growth together and I get to witness a father who supports the emotional development of his children in a way you don't often see. I allow myself to delight, deeply,

deeply delight in my girls as I witness the frivolity and ease they're already experiencing that I didn't have. Cycles of trauma are being broken.

I deliberately and intentionally carved out work for myself that fills my soul. I have the honour and privilege of supporting women to heal their relationship with food so they can begin to come home to themselves. It's the deep and meaningful work my body craved for years.

Every day, I'm increasing my consciousness to be able to respond instead of react. Every decision I make is becoming increasingly more deliberate as I shed the layer of conditioning. This is a million miles away from the young woman on the coach who felt utterly lost and I'm deeply grateful to past me for helping me create this reality.

In the later years of my mom's life, her deepest wish was that her grandchildren didn't experience the trauma she lived and passed down. She spent many years muddling her way through healing intergenerational trauma, years before it was vogue. I 100% believe she did the best she could. Not only did she pave the way for me to do this work, I know she is supporting me still.

BRIANA MCATEER

Briana is a Life Coach and TEDx speaker who has helped hundreds of women around the world to finally heal their relationship with food.

She weaves her passion, endless curiosity and rebel heart to get to the heart of what is TRUE versus what is conditioned, helping women to break-free from the oppressive patriarchal, diet-culture narrative that's kept decades of women stuck on the restrict-binge-shame cycle.

Instead she's calling on women and supporting them to return to the wisdom of their bodies and their own self-leadership so that they can reclaim their confidence and trust around food and feel at HOME in their bodies.

After years of living with a disordered relationship with food, Briana decided she wanted to become a woman who no longer felt controlled by food and was going to learn to honour her body and her health first. In doing so, she not only found emotional freedom from the constant battle with food and weight, but also learned the intricate ways our relationship with ourselves is displayed in our relationship with food. The emotional weight of people pleasing, perfectionism, self-judgement and low self-worth has us reaching for food when we're not hungry and is exactly what she helps her clients overcome.

Becoming a mother to two beautiful girls strengthened her resolve to pursue her mission to help women finally heal their relationship with food; so they can free themselves, but also so they can be the cycle-breakers for generations to come. It is imperative that as women, we can free up the headspace typically consumed with dieting and weight, so that we can dedicate our brilliance to the things that light us up and fuel our families and communities.

This year she is delighted to be embarking on the Somatic Institute for Women's Somatic Educator for Women Certification. She will be deepening her skills in trauma-informed somatic practices and feminine embodiment, which will make her and her coaching all that more powerful.[1]

Briana's Instagram is www.instagram.com/briana.mcateer.coaching

Reference: Rein, V. PHD (2019) *Patriarchal Stress Disorder; the invisible inner barrier to women's happiness and fulfilment.* Lioncrest Publishing (it doesn't give a city). Quote ref. pg.18

YOUR CALLING
HOLLY HOLLAND

My calling is currently at an epidemic level; next only to war and mental health. This is an immense epidemic … and getting worse. It is the epidemic of *Domestic Violence*.

I have often asked myself why this is *my calling,* but I already know the answer. The universe selected me to work on this because I have past and present experience, am compassionate and know how to thrive. For fourteen years, proof of my ability to thrive developed after a personal journey of deep grief, for myself and our young children. It was during the cancer journey and eventual death of my husband, the children's father. I have been successful in creating a new life for us, while keeping his memory alive for our kids who were young when he died from pancreatic cancer. The wonderful, the gut-wrenching and the in between, were all shared with the boys. Encouraging them to continue to live life freely and happily has always been the main idea.

Close personal experience has provided me with ample opportunity to learn, comprehend and understand the impact of *Domestic Violence*. It is a topic that has been prevalent for many generations, in all areas of family and work relationships. People have shared their experiences with me throughout my life. Some sheltered me, while others were blatant about the reality.

People started asking for my help to be a guiding light for them when I was a child, as I was older than my years. Early in adulthood, someone asked what I would change if I could grow up all over again. I said, 'I would be a kid this time.' I do not plan to exercise the kid option, however, I am back after processing everything from a lifetime, initiated by a writing career.

People are completely oblivious of how serious the problem is, and the misunderstanding of it, contributes to the problem. It has become increasingly worse since the pandemic. For some, there is no recognition of the action being wrong; it is like conditioning. The action takers (abusers) are so used to it being a daily part of life, they see nothing wrong. Subtlety plays a huge part.

The action is a topic that people cringe over when they hear the words. I believe it is one of the most misunderstood situations, yet most people know someone who is impacted or have been impacted themselves.

As someone who has been immersed in a wide range of *the action*, it has to stop. We cannot tolerate the behaviour any longer. Solutions are clearly being investigated by people who have no personal experience with it. People overseeing investigations, say changes are being made, but they are also flippant about taking an unlimited amount of time to address the problem, with little to no urgency. There is a lack of understanding of the magnitude of the problem or the danger the recipients are in. Recipients are, in fact, trying to stay alive while changes take so long to come into effect. A critical question is, "how many people need to die for people to understand the magnitude of the problem?"

In my quest to educate people, I defend the recipients of the action, in some way, almost every day. I've noticed that people who are 'helping' them by showing up, removing them from their home temporarily or encouraging them to leave entirely, can sometimes be skeptical of their need for help. They may need proof that the person didn't bring it on themself. Those who don't work in a professional capacity, may not want

125

to get involved, so they don't ask all the questions. When you ask too much, you may hear answers you don't want to hear. However, knowing the *whole truth* is the only way to work towards a solution, as difficult as the answers may be.

It's not unusual, in the current epidemic, for recipients to be assumed to be wrong about some part of the situation: provoking or lying. This is one of the many myths about *the action*. There is never a reason for the action to be taken, at any time.

We must educate to create awareness and understanding of what the action is. The majority of people have some experience with it, although some have experienced it for so long, they do not recognise it. It can be very subtle, especially in public. The action taker does not wish to be caught.

It is important to have people ask questions about anything they do not understand to assist with a solution. Fixing even a small area, in a problem of this magnitude, will begin the process of change and will continue to evolve. Talking about the action will begin to create the knowledge that will help people learn what it is and recognise it when it happens. As we change as a society, and become more vigilant and less tolerant, *the how* will also change.

When the recipients talk, others need to simply listen without judgement. Being open-minded is a wonderful way to support them. They do not wish to be part of it, but often, when in the middle, it is hard to see another way.

Few recipients talk about their situation; most never go to the authorities to report it. Why? Once again, the recipients believe they may not be believed. The most prevalent crime, is when the recipient is not believed, even by some people close to them. The number of incidents reported is extremely small. Each time a person makes a report, they hope they finally will be the one person who will be able to make a huge difference.

One misconception about the action is how it occurs. It can be daily, weekly, monthly, annually or any combination, in any location imaginable. It may stop for long periods of time and improve. When it starts up again, it is generally much more violent. The stops and starts also work against the mindset of the recipient. They often do not know where it is safe, when to speak up or who to talk to. They are tricked into thinking it is over with long periods of absence of activity. The time the action occurs could be any time of the day or night. The time involved ranges from seconds to minutes, hours, days, months and even years.

Another reason action continues, is because of the shame attached to it. The shame keeps the 'wrong people' silent in many cases. Unless there is an active case or a case involving children, we can choose how we address action. If we decide to forgive, that is for us. It is not for the action taker. It is our life, and unless we are currently in a situation, we can freely choose the next step. The next logical step might be to break the silence. This also has a bump in it, as people will avoid speaking up if they think they need to face their abuser. Another reason recipients may not come forward, is the potential impact coming forward could have on other people, like other recipients, their families and even the family of the action-taker. Often the others are already impacted, also afraid to speak up.

The biggest reason people stay silent, is the fear of the action becoming worse, even to the point where their life is taken. Trying to stay alive, with as little impact as possible, becomes their focus.

It is important for us all to believe what the recipients are saying. The large majority have no reason to lie. (There are rare cases of this that jeopardise gains made for the recipients that have told the truth). Less than 10 per cent of accusations are estimated to be false.

For people that operate on a logical basis, action is also hard for people because there is nothing logical about action, therefore there truthfully is never an answer.

All involved need to make every effort to understand the situation of the recipient.

Active cases and suspected active cases - Take immediate action

Stop active incidents through reporting to 911 or police.

Prevent further incidents from occurring with education, awareness, talking, listening and open-mindedness - believe, understand and take action. Promote and utilise anonymous reporting systems and make them available.

Enhance safety measures

Shelters – more physical places to where people can escape, are urgently needed.

Provide financial support to enable leaving the action.

Cases that are not currently active; historical or stable that need processing and support. This is my area of expertise.

Groups – this can be an anonymous member to the group, a name arranged with me to use in the group like chat only, avatar, anonymous format and other innovative ways used, that do not show the identity of participants. Sometimes the anonymous format works - both formats are available.

Applicable to all learning about the action. Each person utilises the techniques they align with.

Journal - Regardless of the timing of when the action occurred, the recipients will let their words and thoughts out in a safe manner. The first place that could be helpful is a journal. It must be kept somewhere others cannot access it. It can be a document on technology - password protected is the best solution. When the place has been determined, start with a pen or keyboard. Write whatever comes to mind. The important thing is to let it out. Go with whatever comes with the writing, keep it flowing. AHA MOMENT … If you write the same thing several times, it needed to be released (times that many). Release the thoughts from your mind to free yourself. You are writing this down for you. The important part is for you simply to *get it out*. The release to the page or the document is freeing.

Meditation – taking time for you, can help all parties clear their thoughts and mind. The value of this practice is tremendous.

Relaxation – this can be of value to all as well. Consider Reiki. Sound bowls, and other energy modalities. Writing your own books - Some of this writing could become a book at some time. This can be determined at a later date.

Domestic violence can be heavy, but it is imperative to educate people, raise awareness, talk about it, listen, be open-minded, believe the recipients, gain an understanding, commit to taking action to stop active incidents, implement safety measures to prevent further incidents from starting and create safety for those who come forward through communication in how we can help ourself, work with people one on one, work with groups, and through writing our story. How all the steps will play out will reveal themselves when the information is needed.

Some of these stories are stuffed away forever, while some keep them for decades. Writing them down and releasing them in a number of ways, like burning them, can help us move on.

The pivotal moment for me was realising the oblivion / generational connection. It is not innocence in the process, rather ignorance; being completely unaware their action is wrong. Thinking a right makes up for a wrong? To be clear on their position, they believe someone can commit domestic violence if there is enough good to balance it out! My question is - *Do they really think that?*

TOP TIPS
- Learn about domestic violence.
- Be aware of the environment of neighbours, co-workers, friends and family. Listen to your inner voice, your intuition.
- If you suspect something is wrong, call 911 or the police.
- Provide the phone number for supports. Many countries have support

numbers. Take a moment to add the support number for your country in the book and to your contacts, if it is not listed here, and keep the number available for easy access.

Canada: - each province has their own help line.

Alberta

Alberta Council of Women's Shelters

(780) 456-700

(866) 331-3933 Hotline

Website: https://acws.ca

Alberta Family Violence Info Line*

(780) 310-1818 Hotline

Website: endfamilyviolence.alberta.ca

*Toll-free, 24/7, Multilingual helpline by phone, text message or chat.

British Columbia

VictimLink BC* (Also serves Yukon)

(800) 563-0808

TTY: (604) 875-0885

Text: (604) 836-6381

Email: VictimLinkBC@bc211.ca

Website: https://www2.gov.bc.ca/gov/content/justice/criminal-justice/victims-of-crime/victimlinkbc

*24/7 help line providing crisis support in 130 languages.

BC Society of Transition Houses

(604) 669-6943

Fax: (604) 682-6962

Email: info@bcsth.ca

Website: https://bcsth.ca/

Ending Violence Association BC

(604) 633-2506

Fax: (604) 633-2507

Website: http://endingviolence.org
Manitoba
Manitoba Association of Women's Shelters
(204) 430-4346
Hotline: 877-977-0007 (24/7)
TTY: (888) 987-2829
Website: http://www.maws.mb.ca/
Newfoundland and Labrador
Transition House Association of Newfoundland and Labrador
(709) 739-6759
Fax: (709) 739-6951
Email: info@thanl.org
Website: http://www.thanl.org
Nova Scotia
Transition House Association of Nova Scotia
(902) 429-7287
Fax: (902) 429-0561
Email: coordinator@thans.ca
Website: http://thans.ca/
Ontario
Ontario Association of Interval & Transition Houses
(416) 977-6619
Email: info@oaith.ca
Website: http://www.oaith.ca/
Assaulted Women's Helpline*
(416) 364-4144
Fax: (416) 364-0563
(866) 863-0511 Hotline
(866) 863-7868 TTY
*Free, confidential counseling, emotional support, safety planning
and referrals for women needing a shelter, legal advice or other supports.

Available 24/7, in more than 100 different languages.

Fem'aide*

(866) 863-0511 Hotline (English)

(866) 863-7868 TTY (English)

(877) 336-2433 Hotline (French)

(866) 860-7082 TTY (French)

Website (English): http://femaide.ca/english/

Website (French): http://femaide.ca/

Talk4Help*

1-855-554-HEAL (4325)

Text: 1-855-554-HEAL

Website: https://www.talk4healing.com/ (live chat available)

*Available in 14 languages.

Quebec

SOS Violence Conjugale*

(514) 728-0023

Fax: 514 728-4247

1-800-363-9010 Hotline (24/7)

(514) 873-9010 Local Hotline (24/7)

Email: sos@sosviolenceconjugale.ca

Website: http://www.sosviolenceconjugale.ca/

*Only province-wide centralized crisis line, 24/7, toll-free, TTY compatible

The Federation of Women's Shelters (FMHF)

(514) 878-9757

Website: http://fede.qc.ca/

Saskatchewan

Provincial Association of Transition Houses and Services of Saskatchewan

(306) 522-3515

Email: paths@sasktel.net

Website: https://pathssk.org

Yukon

VictimLink BC* (Also serves British Columbia)

(800) 563-0808

TTY: (604) 875-0885

Text: (604) 836-6381

Email: VictimLinkBC@bc211.ca

Website: https://www2.gov.bc.ca/gov/content/justice/ criminal-justice/victims-of-crime/victimlinkbc

*24/7 helpline providing crisis support in 130 languages.

United Kingdom: *National Domestic Abuse Helpline* for free and confidential advice, 24 hours

0808 2000 247

Ireland: Tearmann Domestic Violence Services 047 72311

USA: National Domestic Violence Hotline 1-800-799-SAFE (7233)

Australia:

The National Sexual Assault, Family and Domestic Violence Counselling Line

1800 737 732, 24 hours

Austria:

Abuse and Domestic Violence

0800-800-810

hilfswerk.at

You can connect with me here:

hollyroseholland.com

HOLLY HOLLAND

Holly Rose Holland is an intuitive author, grief transition coach, international speaker, former spouse, parent, and grief survivor. While moving through the grief process herself, she noticed that people often become stuck when processing death, difficult relationships, employment-related issues, and even changes within themselves. She practises wellness through nature, and intuition, and travels to share her gifts with the world. "Helping you find your voice." "You will learn so much about yourself as an author."

Holly's first book is called Keep Moving, Creating a Life After Loss (2020, Sapphire Seahorse Press). Having always loved writing, she finds writing to be therapeutic for herself and others, as a means of expressing grief and creating a new life. Best-seller The Business of Connection (2020, ENE) is the first anthology Holly was published in. The Colours of Me (2021, MMH Press) anthology was the next book she was a part of. Holly's novel on domestic violence and a women's fiction book are in editing, publication dates to be announced. A children's book is in the works. This story has been waiting to be told since Holly's childhood.

Holly is passionate about raising awareness of domestic violence, emphasizing the importance of mindset and knowledge.

Holly's website is www.hollyroseholland.com

THE POWER WITHIN
JENNA HASTIE

I started my training as a registered nurse back in 2003 at Glasgow Caledonian University. I absolutely LOVED my career, my vocation and my calling. My last post was THE dream post, working as a trainee Advanced Nurse Practitioner in a General Practice with the most phenomenal team and the nicest patients I have ever worked with!

Now, I specialise in unravelling the underlying causes of autoimmune and chronic diseases. My focus centres on deciphering the hidden triggers that often go undetected by conventional medicine. Some causes are straightforward, like the deficiency of intrinsic factor in pernicious anaemia or the lack of insulin in type 1 diabetes. These are both fixed or irreversible root causes. However, most autoimmune conditions and complex ailments like fibromyalgia and chronic fatigue syndrome, are a mystery to Western medicine. Beyond genetics and chronic stress, researchers are still baffled by their cause.

I'm now going to tell you a story to get you up to speed with my world and how I went about becoming an autoimmune and chronic illness root cause specialist.

Once upon a time, in the not-so-distant past, I found myself trapped in the clutches of mystery symptoms that had taken over my life. The labels of chronic fatigue syndrome, fibromyalgia, anxiety, depression and panic attacks seemed invisible to the exterior world, leaving me feeling isolated and misunderstood. Colleagues didn't believe me and doubts surrounded me like a dark cloud.

I was unwell following the birth of my eldest daughter in 2012 but was fobbed off by my doctors for years. They blamed my tiredness, brain fog, fatigue and back pain on being a new mum. They sent me on my way with a co-codamol prescription. Things marginally improved but my symptoms never fully disappeared. The doctors were happy to continue me on strong codeine - FOR YEARS!

I was knocked for six in 2015 when I discovered I was pregnant with my second daughter. My back and pelvis pain was so severe that I was on crutches, attending weekly physiotherapy. I had to be induced early due to the state I was in. The brain fog and lethargy began to intensify and I also began experiencing migraines for the first time, along with other mysterious symptoms such as high temperatures and tremors. Again, the doctors pawned me off saying I was bound to be feeling off as my husband was working away from home, midweek, and I was solo parenting a 3-year-old and a newborn. Inevitably, the anxiety and depression set in and I began to experience panic attacks and negative and intrusive thoughts.

I was living a demanding life as an Emergency Nurse Practitioner in Accident and Emergency. During one of my shifts, I began experiencing palpitations and an extremely slow heart rate. I was admitted into Cardiology with a heart monitor. They couldn't find any reason for my heart symptoms, despite it registering on the monitors. This is where my journey of diagnosis began.

I was sent to all relevant departments to be assessed – I was even under the care of Infectious Diseases! You honestly couldn't write it. The Infectious Diseases doctor eventually referred me to Rheumatology who diagnosed me with Fibromyalgia and Chronic Fatigue Syndrome. I was prescribed an obscene amount of pain killers, which resulted in me needing other medications to combat the side effects. I was seen by a counsellor and had Cognitive Behavioural Therapy which helped slightly. Things still progressed and my symptoms got worse. The struggle of my conditions and the toll of long hours pushed me to make a pivotal decision. I decided to transition into primary care, where I embarked on a journey as a Trainee Advanced Nurse Practitioner, attending university, once again to study for my master's in advanced practice.

My back pain was unbearable and I began developing problems with my hands and fingers. I was experiencing severe swelling, redness, pain, and stiffness in the affected joints. Again, my GP let me down and brushed things under the carpet. I took matters into my own hands, paying for a private consultation with the man who would soon turn into my Knight in Shining Armour. He listened, he examined and he saw what I saw. He was flabbergasted at how many times I was pawned off regarding my back. You see, my back was a sign … my back had autoimmune arthritis! This doctor became my Rheumatology consultant and if it wasn't for him, I'd hate to think what all my joints would be like today! I was diagnosed in 2019 with a condition called axial spondyloarthritis, an autoimmune disease. While it was a relief to have a name for my new condition, the treatment options offered little comfort. Western medicine operates on an allopathic approach, offering band aid solutions, prescribing multiple medications, to mask my symptoms and more pills to combat side effects. The doctor warned me I had a progressive and lifelong debilitating condition. Things would get progressively worse.

Methotrexate tablets were initially prescribed. Methotrexate is a chemotherapy drug, given to people with certain autoimmune conditions in a much lower dose, over a much longer period, than those with cancer. The tablets made me ill. I was sick as a dog and bed bound. I had to take six tiny methotrexate tablets on a Monday night, and by Tuesday morning, I was vomiting until Friday evening. I literally had a 2-day week! I was prescribed anti-sickness tablets, but nothing seemed strong enough to curb the vomiting. Eventually, I lost a large amount of weight. I was around 7 stone. Bearing in mind that I'm 5ft 6", this was far, far too unhealthy. I was then commenced on methotrexate injections. These were better, but I had to inject myself every Monday and every Tuesday and Wednesday was always a right off.

There wasn't much improvement in my joints, so I was assessed for biologics - these injections cost the NHS a whopping amount of money, so they are means tested. I was quickly commenced on Adalimumab - taken bi-weekly alongside the Methotrexate. The biologics were a breeze compared to the chemo.

The pandemic hit not long after, and it was not safe for me to return to work. My joints on my hand were improving at this point and my back felt AMAZING. However, inflammatory arthritis had spread to my ankle and foot. I was started on another immunosuppressant drug called sulfasalazine. I was on three medications, which combined, completely obliterated my immune system. I was now neutropenic. On top of these immunosuppressants, I was also taking on average 15-20 tablets per day which included pain killers, mood meds and medications to counteract side effects.

Things got depressing again. I was bed bound and had been off work for months and on zero pay. This was my perfect storm. With a heavy heart, I handed in my notice and took myself off the Nursing and Midwifery Council Register - how could I ever go back to my calling in the new world we all now live in? I had no immune system and there were people dying all over the world from Covid. On top of that, I was dealing with chronic pain and symptoms; I was in agony 24/7. My life, as I knew it, was crumbling in front of my eyes. I was overwhelmed, isolated and felt like a prisoner in my own body.

Facing the loss of my nursing career and my half-finished masters', friends left me and I spiralled into a dark place. Thoughts of suicide weighed heavily on my mind, after all, I was living a fate worse than death.

I would daydream for hours, thinking of ways to end things; I finally settled on saving up my medication and taking an overdose. Thankfully, this did not become my reality, as I found a flicker of strength; the love for my husband and two incredible daughters kept me holding on.

In the depths of despair, I stumbled upon the power of mindset and neuroscience practices, capable of rewiring my brain. A spiritual awakening infused me with hope and strength. Lying in bed, I was captivated by visualising playing with my girls outside of that bed. I could hear their laughter in my head and in my mind's eye, I could see the life I so deeply craved. I clung to that vision with every ounce of my being. I repeated this powerful visualisation multiple times every day. During the darkest hours, it became my lifeline.

As I embarked on this journey of self-healing, armed with my extensive medical knowledge and understanding of pathophysiology, I integrated neuroscience, ancient wisdom and spiritual practices, resulting in a transformative synergy emerging. This unique blend empowered me to delve into the realms of mind, body and soul suffering. No longer confined by the limitations of my condition, I became determined to uncover a holistic approach to healing. The fusion of science and spirituality became a beacon of hope and enlightenment for me, reshaping my perspective on my health challenges. It allowed me to view my struggles through a new lens. Opening doors to healing modalities I had never imagined.

As the fog of chronic illness lifted, the powerful interplay between science and spirituality became strikingly evident. My medical knowledge served as a foundation to understand the physical aspects of my conditions, whilst the wisdom of neuroscience and spiritual practices illuminated the intricate connections between my thoughts, emotions, and well-being.

Together, this harmonious integration allowed me to explore the mind, body and soul on a profound level. I was no longer content with band aid solutions and prescriptions that merely masked my symptoms. Instead, I ventured into the unknown. into the depths of self-discovery, seeking the true root causes of my suffering. This is where the 3D healing ™ method was born. Slowly but surely, my joints began to feel lubricated - the stiffness had vanished, the brain fog lifted - I could think clearly now. One by one, my symptoms vanished.

Whilst I was improving, I continued taking my medication. I thought my improvement must have been a combination of everything, but then I'd inject myself with the neon yellow chemo and would be so ill the next day. These medications had to go! One by one I dropped the meds. Eventually, there were no more pills to take except the folic acid and the anti-sickness - these were both needed for the Methotrexate. I stopped all three in one go and continued on the biologics for a few weeks. I was scared to let go of it, but I took my last biologic injection on Tuesday the 27th of April 2021!

As I write this, I am so happy to say that I'm over two and a half years in remission. Medication free. Pain free. Symptom free. This was all achievable by finding the root causes in the mind, body and soul. Thankfully, all of my root causes were reversable. I would like to stress that remission was never what I was aiming for. I never thought it would be possible. I had a chronic and progressive autoimmune disease. All I set out to do, was to gain a better quality of life; a life where I was not bed bound, a life where I could play with my girls, whilst still taking my immunosuppressants and other medications.

Western medicine *is* like a band aid, constantly prescribing medications for symptoms, and prescriptions for side effects. It's a vicious cycle that just doesn't cut the mustard. We need to find the root cause, not put a plaster over symptoms. Now, before the hate police come after me, I do know that Western medicine does have a place, but let's face it, there's room for improvement!

This journey of self-healing not only transformed my life, but ignited a burning desire to share this wisdom with others who are navigating the shadows of chronic illness. I realised my calling extended far beyond the walls of the hospital and the confines of a medical profession. My true purpose lies in guiding others towards their own path of healing and transformation.

The root causes of the mind are limiting beliefs, negative self-talk, childhood wounds and trauma. I would like to stress that every single one of us has childhood wounds and trauma, even those of us who have had, what is deemed, as a perfect childhood. These wounds emerge when our needs are unmet, often stemming from simple feelings of being unheard or unseen. Trauma is not always a catastrophic event either, it can be layers upon layers of stress or conditioning over the years.

The root causes of the body are:

Nutrition. You've heard the saying, "you are what you eat," … it's true.

Leaky Gut Syndrome. I'd like to stress, that if you already have an autoimmune disease, then the likelihood of a leaky gut is astronomical. Seventy to eighty percent of our immune cells are located in the gut. Adrenal fatigue and chronic stress play a significant role. Western medicine is slowly joining the dots here.

A dysregulated nervous system - created due to chronic stress.

And finally, let's look at the root causes of the soul, though I know this may be a new concept for many. Not so long ago, it was for me too. However, we don't only a physical body, but an emotional body and an energy body too. Everything, including us, is composed of energy – a scientific fact. Emotions are energy in motion, and if we don't feel and process them, our emotions lay stagnant, either in our physical, emotional or energetic bodies. We may find we have blockages in our chakras (the energy centres in the body). We may also find ourselves disconnected to our souls. When we lack purpose, this brings about an increase in mental anguish.

Beautiful souls … having shared my journey, my struggles and my triumphs, I want you to remember one thing above all else: *you have an immense power within you*. A power that transcends the labels, the symptoms, the diagnoses and the limitations that life sometimes imposes upon us.

The journey of healing involves synchronising the dimensions of your being – mind, body and soul. It's about recognising the whispers of your body, understanding the stories your emotions tell, and embracing the boundless potential that resides within your spirit. It's about acknowledging that your past experiences, your traumas and your beliefs, do not define you. They are the canvas upon which you can paint your own masterpiece of resilience and strength.

Carry with you the knowledge that you possess the keys to your own healing journey. You have the ability to transform your pain into power, your suffering into strength and your challenges into catalysts for growth.

Remember - the power to heal and to change your reality resides within you. Embrace it, live it and let your light shine brilliantly.

JENNA HASTIE

Jenna Hastie, a beacon of resilience and transformative healing, began her nursing journey in 2003 at Glasgow Caledonian University, where her passion ignited. Her career, a testament to love and dedication, reached its pinnacle as a trainee Advanced Nurse Practitioner in a General Practice, surrounded by an extraordinary team and appreciative patients.

Jenna Hastie's personal journey, a poignant tale of resilience, began in 2012 when mystery symptoms of fatigue, brain fog, lethargy, and migraines took hold. Despite seeking answers, doctors dismissed these concerns, attributing them to the challenges of motherhood. It wasn't until 2016, during her stint as an Emergency Nurse Practitioner, that Jenna finally received diagnoses of chronic fatigue syndrome and fibromyalgia.

Navigating a demanding career, Jenna faced the relentless impact of these conditions. In 2019, while working in primary care as a trainee Advanced Nurse Practitioner, she received the diagnosis of axial spondyloarthritis. The conventional treatments offered little solace, prompting Jenna to forge a unique path to healing, a journey that would lead her to profound self-discovery and transformation.

Her narrative takes a harrowing turn as she confronts the limitations of Western medicine, enduring the side effects of medications and the toll on her body. In the face of debilitating illness, Jenna contemplated the unthinkable but found strength in love and a flicker of hope. A profound shift occurred as she embraced the power of mindset and neuroscience, rewiring her brain and envisioning a life beyond the confines of illness.

Jenna's journey of self-healing seamlessly merged her extensive medical knowledge with neuroscience, ancient wisdom, and spiritual practices. The resulting 3D healing method, a holistic approach addressing the mind, body, and soul, became her lifeline. As she untangled the intricate connections between thoughts, emotions, and well-being, Jenna experienced a remarkable transformation. Her journey to remission, medication-free and pain-free, defied the expectations of a chronic and progressive autoimmune disease.

Emerged from the depths of despair, Jenna's newfound purpose extends beyond hospital walls. Her calling transcends the confines of a medical profession, reaching into the shadows of chronic illness to guide others on their path of healing and transformation. The 3D healing method, rooted in the understanding of limiting beliefs, nutritional imbalances, chronic stress, and the soul's dimensions, offers a beacon of hope.

Transitioning from the conventional path, Jenna embarked on a profound mission—to unravel the mysteries of autoimmune and chronic diseases. With a keen focus on hidden triggers often overlooked by Western medicine, she delved into the complexities of conditions like fibromyalgia and chronic fatigue syndrome. Jenna's expertise extended beyond fixed or irreversible root causes, exploring the enigma that eludes conventional understanding.

Jenna invites others to recognize the immense power within—the power to paint a masterpiece of resilience and strength on the canvas of past experiences. Her message resonates: the journey of healing involves synchronising the dimensions of being—mind, body, and soul. With unwavering conviction, Jenna implores individuals to embrace their ability to transform pain into power and challenges into catalysts for growth.

In the radiant light of Jenna Hastie's journey, she stands as a testament to the inherent power within each individual—a power to heal, to transform, and to illuminate the path to a brighter reality.

Jenna's website is www.jenlogy.co.uk/

CULTIVATE EMOTIONAL INTELLIGENCE
FIONA CONDREN

SAFEGUARD CHILDREN'S MENTAL HEALTH BY CREATING CULTURES OF EMOTIONAL INTELLIGENCE AND SAFETY IN THEIR ENVIRONMENTS.

In 2013, my world came crumbling down, as a result of my teenage daughter's struggles with substance misuse, addiction, mental health, and risk-taking behaviours.

The heartbreak, pain and suffering this caused, combined with a continuing surge in mental health, addiction, self-harm and suicide across both our young and adult population here in my hometown of Derry and throughout Ireland, prompted me to embark on a journey of discovery; a journey to understand why these devastating stories were occurring so frequently and what could be done to affect lasting change.

What I discovered, after many years of research, training, learning, healing and growing, was eye-opening and mind-blowing. This knowledge helped me to understand why I created the life I lived, why I parented the way I did, and why, in some respects, my daughter experienced the challenges she faced, as well as why there is so much pain and suffering in our society.

Armed with this newfound knowledge, despite the adversities and curve balls life has thrown at me, I'm now on a mission to share my teachings with as many people as possible. My aim is to break the cycle of hurt and pain, addressing the pandemics of mental health, addiction, suicide and violence at the core, and creating a better brighter future for our children and future generations.

The fundamental discoveries I uncovered on my journey were:

Within our society, we prioritise IQ. We send children to school for 7 hours a day, 39 weeks a year for 13 to 15 years, but little to no priority is given to EQ – Emotional Intelligence – the ability to be able to identify, understand and manage our emotions in healthy ways.

Emotional Intelligence is a skill. We are not born with it, so if we are not taught, we don't learn.

Not only are we not taught how to understand and manage our emotions in healthy ways, but within our society, emotions are often seen as wrong, inconvenient, or even, inappropriate. As such, we've been taught to shut them down, make them disappear, dismiss them, punish them, and then, after time, try to fix or rescue them. In essence, we don't give children *permission* to feel.

This leads to the suppression of emotions rather than the release of emotions.

When emotions are suppressed, they don't just go away, they show up in two ways: One, outwardly through the use of anger and aggression; the other, inwardly through anxiety and depression. Hence, the pandemics of mental health, violence, crime, domestic abuse and bullying we have on the ground.

Within our society, we make children wrong for displaying any emotion and behaviours outside of what we deem *good*, even though they have undeveloped brains and haven't mastered these skills yet. When we punish and shame children on repeat, the message they hear is, *I'm bad, I'm a problem, there's something wrong with me.* Over time, these messages become beliefs, which then become their blueprint and the core of their being. They grow up to believe they are *not good enough*.

We've been taught to feed children a diet of conditional love. Do what I say, meet my expectations, fill *my* cup, be good, perform/achieve, obey/comply, and I'll give you my love and attention; if you don't, I'll withdraw it.

We have been taught to use children's greatest needs for unconditional love and acceptance against them, to get them to think, feel, behave and be who *we want them to be*.

We have been taught to raise children in environments where love and fear go hand in hand, clouding their judgement of what love really is. This then sets the blueprint for all future relationships.

So, how we have been taught to raise children impacts their emotional, physiological and social well-being, which are the three critical components of mental health.

Our childhood creates and shapes the life we live in adulthood. As a result of how most of us have been raised, we all carry some form of pain from our childhood; some greater than others, depending on circumstances.

Pain from not being given permission to feel our feelings.

Pain from having to suppress those emotions and keep them stuffed down inside.

Pain from not feeling safe to be our true authentic self.

Pain from having to disconnect from ourselves and keep parts of us hidden.

Pain from having to develop survival coping mechanisms.

Pain from wearing various masks and not knowing who we are.

Pain from being constantly triggered because of our wounds and invisible scars.

Pain from not being taught how to understand and healthily manage our emotions.

Pain from having to carry that dynamic.

Pain from having to run, avoid, mask, numb and suppress.

Pain from being made wrong for expressing our feelings and needs, in the only way we knew how.

Pain from being punished, shamed and criticised.

Pain from feeling that we weren't good enough.

Pain from feeling that we always had to prove ourselves.

Pain from not having experienced the unconditional love, safety and security we needed.

Pain from the sheer exhaustion of having to carry all that shite around with us on a day-to-day basis.

What then happens, is that we bring all this to the table when we become parents ourselves. Without even knowing, we pass our hurt, pain and wounds onto the shoulders of our children. That's how these inter-generational cycles continue.

Many of us, because of how we've been wired, combined with our inability to regulate our emotions, project and mirror that onto our children; our state determines their state. It doesn't feel safe to them, and as a result, our children are wired with stress and fear, which doesn't grow a healthy brain, and so, the cycle continues.

Here in Northern Ireland, this has been further compounded because of the conflict, war and troubles, which are clearly reflected in the statistics here around mental health, addiction, suicide and domestic violence. When we look back to the late 1960s, when our parents were children and teens, not only were they brought up in behavioural environments where it wasn't safe to express their feelings, but they also had to endure the additional stress associated with the environments around them. Outside of their home, the streets were filled with carnage, rioting, bombing, sniper attacks, people being shot dead in broad daylight, and mass murders on both sides of the community. Amongst all this, they were not taught how to manage their feelings or develop coping mechanisms, not because of any wrongdoing on their parent's part, but because this knowledge wasn't available to them.

These environments contributed to creating their minds. That was their reality. That was their normal. In hindsight, however, there was nothing normal about it. It was traumatic, dysfunctional, fear-driven and totally abnormal. What did become normal, though, was the fact that fight and/or flight became the baseline for many. They became stuck in an ingrained dysregulated state and had to find survival mechanisms to cope. They then passed that onto the shoulders of their children .... and the cycle continued.

So, whilst the war may have ended on the outside, Ireland will never truly be at peace until we address the invisible wounds and scars left behind and teach people how to regulate their emotions in healthy ways. Our people deserve that - given what they've come through. Credit to them for raising us all in the best way they knew how, despite the challenges and adversities they faced.

But, until we afford them this opportunity, the war will continue to live on, internally within us, one generation after another.

Reflecting on my own life whilst on this journey, I clearly remember the evening when I was piecing together all the information and knowledge I'd acquired, putting the pieces of the jigsaw together. I got an overwhelming feeling in my body. Instead of doing what I had previously done and pushing it away, I welcomed the feeling in and listened to what it was telling me. But nothing prepared me for the discovery I was to make - which was that *I was dysfunctional.*

This is not a word we would ever use to describe ourselves; well, it certainly wasn't for me, given that I'd spent a lifetime perfecting the opposite to the outside world.

Initially, I was shocked, but I didn't let my ego get in the way. I didn't dismiss the thoughts in my head because that would have defeated the purpose of what I was trying to achieve.

This was no longer about me. I had a daughter who suffered immensely, and I was now raising another daughter.

I needed to understand what role I was playing in that. I raised my daughter. I created the environments around her. I was responsible for growing her brain. To affect change for my children and break these cycles of hurt/pain, I needed to shine the spotlight inwards on myself. I needed to be honest, irrespective of how challenging that may be, and to do that, I had to accept this was my reality. *I was dysfunctional.*

I couldn't function effectively.

I was flawed and messed up.

I couldn't regulate my emotions.

I stuffed them down inside.

I often felt anxious, fearful, panicky and scared.

I developed survival coping mechanisms.

I wore multiple masks.

I took on everyone's problems and feelings because I couldn't cope with my own.

I was a fixer.

I was a people pleaser.

I sought validation from others.

I was always looking to my daughter to fill my cup.

I found it difficult to put boundaries in place.

I neglected my own needs.

But despite all of this, I was a master performer. Despite my internal struggles, I had crafted the art of perfecting to the outside that all was *good* in my world.

After four decades, there it was as clear as day - *my life was just a big showcase, a pretence.*

Things exacerbated further after the birth of my second daughter. What was supposed to be an exciting chapter of our life, turned into one of the biggest heartbreaks and struggles I had ever had to endure. After a normal pregnancy, to be told that my daughter was brain damaged, resulting in her being significantly disabled with a life-limiting condition, was soul-destroying.

The mammy who went into hospital to have my daughter wasn't the mammy who returned weeks later.

I was lost and broken. I was hurt, scared, frightened, anxious, stressed and overwhelmed. I couldn't cope with the enormity of the thoughts and feelings I was experiencing. I remember thinking, *Why me? Why my child? This isn't what I asked for. I don't have what it takes to do this; this isn't how I expected my life to play out.* Then I felt guilty and ashamed, but of course, I pushed those feelings down and kept myself busy, so I didn't have time to think and feel. I felt so out of control within myself that I tried to control everything around me. Life was like a production factory; going through the motions every day like a robot. Breakfast, school, homework, work, hobbies, showers, dinner. It was all about the 'doing' without being present, conscious and connected.

Again, to the outside world, it appeared as though I was coping well. Professionals called, the house was cleaned, I looked well, the girls looked well, but after they left, I often looked at my wee daughter and thought, *She'll never walk; she'll never talk. She will always suffer and never be able to tell me how she is feeling.* My heart was shattered in a thousand pieces, resulting in me spending a long number of years in fight/flight, even after the birth of my third daughter.

That was the environment in which I was raising my children, so now it made sense why my eldest daughter had suffered so much.

I couldn't cope with my emotions.

I projected and mirrored them onto her.

I was lost and broken.

She was lost and broken.

She communicated this story to me through her behaviour.

I was led to believe this was misbehaviour, so instead of *responding* to her needs, I *reacted* to her behaviour.

I didn't see her, hear her or understand her.

I saw her as a problem … and she felt that.

At possibly the most vulnerable stage of her development, when her body and brain was undergoing immense changes, she needed me to catch her and keep her safe, but in effect, I turned my back on her.

I used fear, punishments and shame, anything to make the 'bad behaviour' go away. I should have seen this as a cry for help, but because of my lack of knowledge, and the fact that I was so disconnected from myself, I couldn't provide her with the safety and security she needed.

When my daughter's needs weren't met in that relationship with me, she sought to get them from outside of the home. Alcohol and drugs soothed her because I didn't. Substances met the needs I didn't respond to because I reacted to the behaviour. They numbed the hurt, pain, rejection and loneliness. Over time, this took its toll on her mental health, causing immeasurable suffering.

So, the harsh reality is, *my daughter was never the problem*. It was me. That's when my inner work started. Healing my own wounds; dealing with the loss and grief of not having an able-bodied child, accepting my beautiful wee daughter for who she was, ending my marriage, (which should have ended many years previously), reprogramming my mind, learning how to regulate my emotions, changing my parenting style, and finally learning to be the person my girls needed me to be.

The hard truth is, I *unintentionally* damaged my daughter's developing brain and her self-identity. This resulted in her being wired up in survival mode. If only I knew then what I know now, how I would have done things differently. But this knowledge wasn't available to me back then.

I can't go back and change the past, but I can use my knowledge *now*, to impact the future. I can use my story to educate and inspire others to affect change, so we can end these generational cycles of trauma, hurt and pain, and in doing so, give every child the future they deserve.

The key takeaways from my story and teachings are:

We must raise children in the way nature always intended, with unconditional love and acceptance, before societal conditioning and programming got in the way.

We must remove fear, control and punishments from how we raise and parent children.

We must see behaviour as communication and learn to respond to children's needs rather than react to the behaviour.

We need to treat children with the same respect and dignity we would any other adult we are in a relationship with, and to do that, we must change the toxic narratives we have within our society around how we view children, emotions, behaviours, parenting and discipline.

We must heal our own wounds and learn how to regulate our emotions, so we can show and teach children how to do the same.

As a society, we must prioritise emotional Intelligence, with the current research available. Not teaching our children how to identify, understand and manage their emotions in healthy ways, is one of the biggest tragedies of our time.

We must ensure that when children are ready to leave home, they can cope with their emotions healthily; they are resilient, emotionally intelligent, can problem solve, manage conflict, and have self-confidence, self-esteem, self-respect and self-love.

We must make our generation the last generation of wounded children in adult bodies. Otherwise, we will continue to treat the symptoms of addiction, mental health, violence, and suicide because hurt people hurt people … but people who love themselves don't hurt themselves or others.

So, let's infuse as much love and safety into those little humans as we can, so that by the time they leave home, they can infuse that love onto themselves and others.

Remember that our children come into the world whole and complete, so why do many end up wounded, damaged, broken, addicted and 'sick'?

It's predominately because of how we have been taught to raise them. It's because of how we have been conditioned and programmed and what we then download onto them, which creates their minds.

But the good news is:

We, the big people, can change that.

We can now follow the science.

We can now affect change.

When we change, everything changes.

That's how we change the world for our children.

FIONA CONDREN

"*We will never address the pandemics of mental health, violence and suicide unless we change the toxic narratives we have within our society around children, emotions, behaviour, parenting and discipline.*" *Fiona Condren, Emotions Matter*

Fiona Condren is on an unstoppable mission to change the world for our children by teaching their big people to understand what it is they need, so they get the opportunity to grow up to be healthy, secure and emotionally intelligent adults in the world.

Mother of 3 girls. Fiona is an experienced Parent Coach, Educator, Emotion Coach Practitioner Trainer and a Qualified Social Worker; working with families, community and organisations for almost 30 years.

Fiona authentically shares her own inspirational story of overcoming family life challenges, including the heartbreak and struggle she encountered whilst raising her own teenager daughter, with no map or compass at that time.

After a continued surge of mental health and suicide in her own hometown of Derry and throughout Ireland, as a whole. Fiona embarked on a journey of discovery to understand why these devastating stories were occurring so frequently and what could be carried out to affect lasting change.

What she discovered was both mind-blowing and eye opening.

The golden nugget for Fiona was that Emotional Intelligence is the missing agenda in our society, she discovered:

We don't give children permission to feel.

We don't teach them how to manage their emotions in healthy ways.

We make them wrong for displaying any emotions outside of what's deemed to be good, despite the fact that they have an underdeveloped brain and haven't mastered these skills yet.

All of which impacts on their emotional, psychological and social well-being. So, in essence how we have been taught to raise children impacts on their mental health, far from bringing them home to their true selves in the world.

Armed with this newfound knowledge, research and training combined with her own experience both professionally and personally, she embarked to bring this out in the open and break generational cycles and Emotions Matter was borne.

Within the first year of business Fiona gained regional recognition when she was awarded runner up in the Entrepreneur of the Year Award NI 2022.

Fiona has helped countless big people up and down the country to transform how they parent, teach and work with children. She is well renowned for her certainty and reliability in supporting families that are actively struggling or in crisis and turns the story around.

Fiona not only educates, she empowers and inspires her audiences and clients. Many have described her talks, training and presentations as both fascinating and intriguing and she gets result, leading real change being affected on the ground and cycles beginning to break.

Fiona is passionate, energetic, and enthusiastic. She's a cycle breaker, game changer and a powerhouse. Trailblazing, Fiona firmly believes at the core of her being that if the big people take action and re-educate themselves, together, we can rewrite this script and in doing so change the world for our children because their emotions matter.

Fiona's Facebook is www.facebook.com/emotionsmatterni

WHAT MIGHT BE POSSIBLE
IF YOU DARED TO BELIEVE?
CLAIRE AUCHMUTY

On a recent Thursday morning, I boarded an EasyJet flight in Belfast International Airport and flew to London Stanstead. From there, I took the Stanstead Express into Liverpool Street Station and hopped on a tube, travelling just two stops to St Paul's Cathedral. This trip would be a combination of both business and pleasure, and that day I was meeting a friend who I had trained with, and who worked directly opposite St Paul's. As I exited the tube station, I stepped about four paces onto the street and literally stopped dead in my tracks. I had such a tangible sense of space ... and of being able to breathe. I'm sure I caused a backlog of people behind me as they came up the steps out of the tube station, but at that moment, I didn't care. I was aware of so many sounds around me; the buses, the cars, people on bicycles, people talking, music coming from different directions, hustle and bustle on all sides. As I stood on this non-descript street in the centre of London, I realised that for the first time, in quite a long time, I could breathe deeply and easily. Suddenly, I had a very strong sense of who I was.

It felt good on that Thursday morning, just being able to decide to hop on a plane without having to ask anyone's permission. I was 17 months into working full time in my business as a Professional Divorce and Relationship Coach. I still loved the novelty of being able to create my own diary. As I stood there on the street, I thought *I know who I am*. I'm a business owner, I'm a mum to two amazing boys, I'm a sister, a friend, and a mentor. I am kind, generous, loving life and I'm ready to take risks; to move forward knowing I am the only person in the world who can actually move my life forward. Most important of all, I knew I could feel hope; hope for the future. And this was drawing me forward into something that felt bigger than me, more expansive and quite exciting.

But this wasn't always who I was. This wasn't always the life I had lived. I'd love you to become curious for a minute: Have you ever felt this sense of space? This sense of being able to breathe? Where was it? When was it? What had been going on around you at the time? Would you like to feel it again?

Let me bring you back to where I was in life, less than eight years earlier. I'd like you to imagine me getting into bed on a cold, blustery, wet winter's evening. My electric blanket is on, I have a steaming cup of tea beside the bed and my two boys, aged four and six, are asleep in bunk beds in the room next door. I pick up a book from my bedside locker, one I had just bought on the topic of divorce and start to read.

In the first chapter, the author discusses change and how, on a divorce journey, change impacts every part of life as it was once experienced. This concept I understood well, having just two weeks earlier stepped out of a marriage, that from my perspective, was broken beyond repair. I had left our family home and moved into an apartment.

The second chapter, however, became more challenging for me. In this chapter, the author talked about identity, and described how every person on a divorce journey, regardless of the reason for the split, who was to blame, and indeed which side you happened to be on, needed to find a new identity.

At this point, I put the book down and stare into the distance. I haven't got the first clue what to do with the words I have just read. Lots of questions start to jump out at me. How does anyone find a new identity? Where do you start? What is my identity?

I knew a few things about my identity; I knew I was a mum, a nurse, a daughter, a sister, a friend. But I was also very aware of the fact that I was no longer a wife, no longer living as a family of four under one roof, no longer married to a church minister, and yet, at that time, neither was I divorced. I was kind, generous, had a strong faith and yet no longer had a sense of fun, balance, calmness, or connection. I felt I was living in limbo, and for this I had no reference point.

The reality of my life on that winter's night, I remember so well. I remember the emotions of fear, loneliness, upset, judgement, unfairness, feeling overwhelmed, responsibility, exhaustion, anger, a sense of chaos and having no solid ground beneath my feet. As if this major life event wasn't enough in my world, just three weeks earlier my career had changed direction. I had chosen to leave the nursing management team in my local Emergency Department where I had worked for the previous 10 years. I stepped into my new role as a Respiratory Practice Nurse in a GP surgery, started a respiratory diploma, despite not having studied for 15 years: talk about feeling like a fish out of water. Yes, I definitely felt that I grasped the concept of change alright!

We know every journey starts with a single step, and by the time I was getting into bed on that January night, I felt I had already climbed Mount Everest, single-handedly, with no training. Yet this was only the very beginning. I knew enough to know that in order *not* to stay in the place I have described, I was the only one who could do anything about it. So, step by step, slowly at first, with lots of ups and downs, and many a detour along the way, I have navigated my way from that bedroom in January 2016, into the life I live in now. A life in which I have clarity, connection, direction, and purpose. I have changed my career pathway and stepped away from nursing completely. I am currently the CEO of my own business, *Claire Auchmuty Coaching*, where I have the honour and privilege of walking alongside others as they navigate their own relationship breakdowns.

I mentioned earlier the idea of a reference point, which for me is a standard by which to gauge a situation or event. I quite like the symbolism of a lighthouse as it is strong and solid and has definite purpose. The purpose of a lighthouse is to keep the ships safe, illuminating danger, guiding them safely past the rocks and the dangers they don't see within the waters around it.

So, what I have discovered by reflecting back over my life, is that my general reference point for change is knowing quite solidly what I do not want. I changed my nursing direction from an Emergency Department into that of a GP Practice because I no longer wanted to work night duty or weekends. Most of all, what I really didn't want was for my children to grow up hearing their mum say, "I'm tired" or "I'm going to work". The journey to have our amazing boys included multiple failed IVF cycles, miscarriages, and then further holistic interventions, and this wasn't what I wanted them to have as their childhood memories.

In very much the same way, when I was reflecting on my marriage and my experience of it, I realised that whilst I didn't know exactly what I wanted, there were certain things I knew I didn't want any more. I didn't want to keep feeling the hamster wheel of the same issues with no real lasting change. Somehow, no matter what we tried to put into practice, dynamics between us seemed to remain the same, so when I knew what it was that I didn't want, I did a 180-degree turn. I didn't know what I actually wanted or even *needed* in my future, but my reference point was very solid; I did not want this, and of that I was very sure. Just as the lighthouse alerts a ship of underlying danger, it is the ship's captain who must take action, and steer the vessel away. And I too, was sure my path must take a different course.

Quite often in life change comes in one of two ways; a single event that we can always pinpoint back to, or it is the proverbial "straw". In my experience, the second makes the decision to change much more difficult. It can be hard to articulate our reasons for change to other people when they may have no awareness of the reality of our life. Yet the accumulation can become too much, as was the case for me.

At that point in my life, I began to understand that the only person or situation I could control was myself. Years later, I now have a much better understanding, that as humans, we have full responsibility for our thoughts, our feelings, our actions, our decisions, and our attitudes, and that we are not responsible for, nor can we control, any other human being on the planet.

In 1997 when I got married, I not only became a wife, but I became a church minister's wife. Effectively, I gained 2 new roles within my identity at the one time. Over my 19 years of marriage, we moved parish three times, which meant each time we had a geographical change of location, as well as a complete change of our support structure and people within our world. Alongside these changes, I had also changed my job - both in role and location, four times. Each job change generated a new identity as I moved though the nursing grade scales into a management position. Something I was vaguely aware of over this time, but didn't really understand, was how inextricably linked the journeys of change and grief are. Every change in our lives brings both loss and something new. Some changes we plan for and some changes we find ourselves in the middle of, wondering how on earth we got to be where we are.

What I began to realise in the apartment during the months following my marriage breakdown, was that whilst I had experienced lots of changes in my life up to that point, and in my humble opinion I felt I had navigated them fairly well, in this journey of change I was struggling to find the ground beneath my feet.

I became curious about this concept of a new identity that the author of the book had raised. I realised that in stepping out of both my marriage and my familiar nursing role almost at the same time, I had lost multiple identities all at once. It's no wonder I felt lost, lonely and, quite honestly, all over the place.

Looking back with the benefit of hindsight on this time in my life, I realise there was a frequent misconception that because I had chosen to leave, I must be okay. After all, it was my decision. Yet this was very far from the truth in the reality of my world. What further didn't help me, was that I was very independent and capable and had no idea how to ask for help or indeed identify what I might actually have needed. This became a barrier that kept me isolated and disconnected. Without a doubt, the most challenging part of my divorce journey was becoming vulnerable and seeing this as a strength.

Brene Brown, an American professor who has spent her life being curious about vulnerability, shame, and empathy, says that "vulnerability is the birthplace of love, belonging, joy, courage, empathy and creativity." When I read that for the first time, it really didn't resonate with me because it was so unfamiliar, whereas now, many years later, I am living the truth of these words.

I began to read books, watch YouTube videos, go to therapy, and search the internet to learn more about why I was feeling the way I was. My default question always seemed to be "what's wrong with me?". I found myself time and again feeling overwhelmed and unable to make decisions. The idea that this could be "normal" was alien to me.

My journey into vulnerability started with the awareness that my two most frequent questions to myself were, "What's wrong with me?" as I've mentioned, and "How on Earth do I do this?" Over time I figured they might not be the most helpful questions as they created thought loops that seemed to have no exit points. As I read and understood more of Brene Brown's work, I also came across a wonderful book that generated another lightbulb moment for me. In the book, *Who Not How* by Dan

Sullivan and Dr Benjamin Hardy, they discuss the concept of instead of asking, "How" to do something, switch the question to "Who do I know who can help?". This change of question opened up my thought pathways to find answers outside the familiar patterns and boxes that were my comfort zone. It began to unlock something in me, as I realised that maybe, some things didn't have to be as hard as I was making them.

It was over this time that the idea of my life as a story started to enter my thoughts, and I linked it directly to the concept of identity. I decided my identity was more to do with how I saw myself rather than how other people saw me, and this was an aspect that I hadn't become curious about before.

I started to author my own story and, bit by bit, my confidence began to grow. Firstly, as I've mentioned previously, by knowing what I didn't want (almost like a launch pad), figuring out what might be possible and then what I might actually want. Slowly, but surely, I began to feel an excitement rising deep within, as I realised I could decide what got to stay in my story, what got to be added, and what I could choose to let go of. I began to add in more fun and adventure and make more memories. I took my dad and the boys on holidays, went to concerts, set up a new home, and quite liked the outcomes of the decisions I was making.

My greatest learning on this journey from that apartment bedroom to the life I live now, has been the understanding that at any given time, I only need to know my next right step. Not the plan, not the end result, not the roadmap - as these are all factors which have the potential to generate overwhelm and bring me back to a place of feeling stuck.

I now know the feeling of hope as it draws me forward and understand, it is in my taking the action for my next right step, that takes me there.

On that note I'd love to leave you, the reader, with a question:

What might be possible for you, if you dared to believe your story mattered?

CLAIRE AUCHMUTY

C laire Auchmuty is a Professional Divorce and Relationship Coach, whose mission revolves around helping individuals navigate tumultuous relationships and find clarity in the midst of emotional turmoil. She is dedicated to assisting those grappling with the age-old question of *should I go, should I stay?* Claire firmly believes that uncovering the intricate dynamics beneath these dilemmas can unlock the door to a brighter, more empowered future.

Claire's journey into coaching was deeply rooted in her own divorce experience, marked by emotional upheaval, uncertainty and transformation. Drawing from these trials, she realised the potential in helping others navigate similar terrain and decided to make it her mission to offer profound insights, wisdom and guidance for those seeking relationship resolution.

With over three decades of nursing experience, including an impressive thirty-six-year career in both Paediatrics and Emergency Medicine, Claire brings a unique blend of skills and empathy to her coaching practice. Her expertise extends beyond understanding human emotions; she approaches each situation with an analytical and compassionate eye, recognising that the path to clarity requires emotional support and a methodical approach, making her an ideal companion during times of relationship turmoil.

Claire's coaching style is built on empathy, intuition and the belief in the power of questions to illuminate the path forward. She asks questions that open up uncharted vistas in her clients' minds, enabling them to discover choices they may not have known existed. Gaining clarity and understanding can open up a world of possibilities.

Recognising that each person's relationship struggles are unique and deserve a personalised approach, Claire tailors her coaching to the specific needs and dynamics of her clients, ensuring they not only find answers but embark on a journey of self-discovery and empowerment. Her nursing background allows her to approach clients with care, respect and professionalism, creating a safe space for them to explore their feelings and thoughts.

Claire has witnessed the transformation that occurs when her clients emerge from confusion and uncertainty with new-found clarity. With her support, they make conscious decisions and chart a course towards healthier, happier relationships or gather the strength to embark on a new chapter in life.

Her unique blend of life experience, professional training and innate empathy positions Claire as a powerful ally for anyone facing relationship turmoil. She doesn't just offer answers; she helps individuals discover the questions that empower them to change their lives. Claire's journey, experiences and commitment to guiding others through relationship challenges form the foundation of her coaching practice.

Claire's website is www.claireauchmutycoaching.com

LEARNING TO LET GO
MAIREAD McDONALD

What does unstoppable mean to me?

Unstoppable means overcoming whatever barriers are put in your way. No matter what, you will keep going – and not stop. Nothing can stand in her way, no matter who tries to stop her. A defiance. A determination. A resilience. An inner strength. An inner power. A story of overcoming, a story of becoming.

Am I unstoppable? I feel like I am now, but I didn't always feel this way.

One thing that definitely stopped me, was a shoulder injury. A rotator cuff tear while I was living in Perth, Australia in 2017. It made me stop in my tracks. I stopped working. I stopped exercising every day. I stopped driving … and dating … and partying. I stopped drying my own hair, chopping my own vegetables, changing my own bedclothes. I stopped living the best life I could imagine.

It was a workplace injury, sustained from a risk I had identified the day before. There I was, in a workers' compensation claim, three months in, and counting. I was in a colossal amount of pain, with an immobile shoulder, and extensive referred neck and back pain. No one knew what was wrong with me. I was stopped in my tracks.

I had lost count of the number of x-rays, ultrasounds and MRI scans I was sent to. It was St Patrick's Day, which is not a Public Holiday in

Western Australia, and I was on the bus with my mum's school friend, going to find out if the latest MRI scan produced any tangible results. At that stage, I was being tested for MS. I worked as a Disability Support Worker across many agencies and organisations in the Perth Metropolitan Area, including the MS Society. I knew and understood the debilitating effects MS would bring. Was this to be my fate? The words of the Workers Compensation Case Handler echoed through my mind; "if this test comes back clear as well, will you consider the possibility that this has all been in your head, that it's a psychosocial pain?" I know I loved the chat and to talk about how I was feeling, but had I really created this debilitating pain and discomfort because of how I was thinking and feeling? Had I finally lost it? I was about to find out.

The test was clear. I didn't have MS. But before they consigned me to the asylum, I requested one thing: "Can someone please check my shoulder? That's where my pain started three months ago, and I still get sore using it."

Within two weeks, I was on the operating table. I was assessed and scanned, and they found a 9mm tear in the right rotator cuff. I wasn't losing it, after all. I had a tear in my shoulder. It explained the pain, the immobility of the shoulder, and the referred neck and back pain. I had spoken up for myself … and finally I had an answer.

For years, I remember *not* speaking up for myself. Being spoken over in groups. Wanting to talk but the words wouldn't come out. I have had a stutter for as long as I can remember. It's barely noticeable most days as a 40-year-old woman, but as a child, it stopped me from talking easily at home and at school. It stopped me from telling my stories and jokes, from sharing ideas and opinions. I was feeling and thinking everything but couldn't express it quick enough to keep up with the flow of the conversation. Some people call a stutter a stoppage, and that's how I felt as a child; stopped.

Fast forward to 2024 and I facilitate wellness groups for parents. I talk openly and honestly in groups. I give talks and facilitate workshops. *I literally talk for a living.* I share my tried, tested and trained techniques for parents to nurture themselves every single day, and teach the wellbeing tools to their kids.

I have one son, a 4-year-old boy called Francis, named after my deceased brother, who died in 2003. Francis really is *my why*.

He is the reason I continue to heal and bring out the best in myself, every single day. He deserves the best of me. And I vow to teach him everything I know about how to nurture and take care of his own wellbeing.

It turns out our bodies can store unprocessed emotions as bundles of energy, and these bundles of energy can cause pain and disease. That's what happened to my shoulder.

My very painful shoulder injury was caused by trapped grief from my brother dying, thirteen years prior to my injury. An energy healer was able to tell me that. A very beautiful and talented lady called Louise Byrne from Waterford, Ireland. We met when I lived in Perth and I continued a healing journey with her for many years afterwards. Louise was a Godsend and someone I later went on to study Usui Reiki Level 1, Level 2 and Reiki Masters with.

Louise was able to clear the trapped emotion of grief within my shoulder. Through a year's difficult physical rehabilitation, I began to build up movement and functionality in my shoulder again; I developed some fitness and strength again. I built my own bed a year after my shoulder operation - I was coming back. And I never wanted to go through anything like that again.

2017 was an absolute life changing year for me. I learned that a trapped emotion could cause a great deal of pain. I vowed I would learn to process my emotions better in the future. All of that pain, was because I didn't know how to handle my feelings and emotions in a healthy way.

And so, equipped with this enthusiasm for self-awareness, Louise taught me to meditate. I had never meditated before, and thought it was something hippies do, but I was willing to become a hippie if it meant never going through that year again. So, I listened. And I practised what I was taught.

I remember going to the beautiful Kings Park in Perth with a page in my pocket. It contained the words:

Acknowledge

Process

Release

Replace

This was to become a very simple and extremely effective tool I still use today, and now teach in my 6-week wellness coaching course for parents.

ACKNOWLEDGE

Quite simply, acknowledge the emotion. Give it a name. Label it. I called mine frustration.

PROCESS

Let yourself feel it in every cell of your body. Let it be. Give it space. Feel that frustration.

RELEASE

This means *let it go*. I released down through the soles of my feet onto the grass below me. You can breathe it out, move it out, shake it out, dance it out, hum it out, in whatever way you choose - just let it go.

REPLACE

Replace it with something else. Choose another emotion you do want to feel. I chose acceptance; of my situation, of my still recovering shoulder, of my somewhat still limited capacity to fully engage in the Perth lifestyle I knew and loved. Acceptance of where I was in my recovery.

This very simple four step approach to 'deal with' my emotions was a revelation to me for a number of reasons.

Permission to feel:

It gave me permission to feel. To acknowledge and feel the emotion I felt and watch as it passed - without judgement. E-motions are energy in motion. And it takes as little as 90 seconds for the energy of an emotion to pass through us, when we just allow it to be.

So much of our Irish cultural conditioning is about suppressing emotions… "oh have a drink and forget about it", "don't feel that", "don't cry", "you've nothing to cry about", "look on the bright side" or "someone else has it worse than you." So many ways our experience and emotions are invalidated.

I remember one of my primary drives to study an Honours Psychology Degree in the Queen's University of Belfast, was to understand the human condition, my human condition. My now-deceased brother, Francis, was the cheeriest, most positive, bubbly, drolly, dry-witted, accepting person I knew. We were very close. He had a life-limiting condition called Duchenne Muscular Dystrophy and knew he would die young. He asked questions, he gained understanding, and he accepted his fate. While I, "with nothing to complain about", was a down and depressed teenager. How I wish I had Louise's 4 step approach to processing emotions back them! But in 2002, I started Queen's to study Psychology, the scientific study of the mind and behaviour. And I learned about individual differences, the nature nurture debate, and many other things which helped me to understand and validate my experience.

Suppression of emotions and experiences is very real. Sometimes, emotions are just too big or difficult to process. We often don't understand what we're feeling or have the words to describe it or explain it. We may not have the right support around us. People aren't reared with an awareness and knowledge about how to handle the big feelings we all feel. And so, it can be very easy to distract ourselves from what we are truly feeling, to numb the feeling and the pain. As humans, we do this in a number of ways, by zoning out, by overworking, by over-achieving, overeating, over-drinking, escapism through the tv, phone, drugs, alcohol, gambling, porn, shopping… this list is not exhaustive. While some of those activities, in very small amounts, can be healthy, they can become a distraction for what is really going on.

Releasing

The realisation that I could *let things go*, was a major light bulb moment for me. Emotions are allowed to go. I don't have to hold onto, cling or attach to anything I feel or experience. When my stutter eased with age, I became the best girl around for talking about what was going on, what happened to 'make me feel' this way, the chain of events, the story, "he said this, I said this, she said this, imagine! Can you believe it?"

While social connection and support is very important and necessary for human survival, we can often get lost in 'the story' of what happened and how it happened. I didn't know how to let anything go.

When we talk about and think about something that has happened in our lives, our bodies don't know if this is happening now or if it happened in the past, so we can feel the same emotions we felt in the lived experience. I find writing the best way for me to process my emotions, feelings and share my story. There are times when the writing I did got burned, if it was a release of some very difficult emotions and experiences. While at other times, I enjoyed reading over my writing, reflecting, processing and acknowledging what was going on for me at the time.

Believe me when I say, with the right support, some very difficult emotions and experiences can be worked through, acknowledged, processed, released and replaced. Sometimes the things we're holding onto, the belief patterns we have adopted, are too much to take on alone. And that's ok. There is plenty of help out there to release some bigger emotions and stresses, dealing with the experiences and stories held within the body. I have used a wide variety of disciplines. In the early days with grief, it was counselling and then after the shoulder injury, I progressed to energy healing, kinesiologists, reiki, acupuncture, and reflexology.

Replacing

Replacing emotions felt very empowering for me. I forgot I had a choice in how I was feeling. I didn't have to let my emotions run the show. It is a choice; an active, proactive, empowering choice.

Someone who understood this, was my mother. Mammy knew we had a choice in how we felt and what we did. When I was 16, I wondered why I wasn't feeling any different after taking prescribed antidepressant tablets for a few weeks. Mammy's response to me was; "There's a lot you can do to help yourself."

"Really, Mammy? Is there? Will a tablet not fix me?"

"No Mairead, it won't."

"What can I do to help myself Mammy?"

"You can take a bath, go for a walk, drink some water, eat a piece of fruit, read a book, do some colouring in that you like. Do things that are good for you, going down home helps me."

Mammy knew what self-care was, without calling it self-care. She knew how to replace what you're feeling with something else by doing something that's good for you.

Anyone who has ever experienced CBT counselling will understand this model:

CBT is based on the principle that we think affects how we feel and act. CBT is focussed on acknowledging, processing, challenging and changing our thinking patterns, in order to change how we feel and act. This model can also be used to create change by taking action to acknowledge process, release and replace our emotions or to change the actions we are taking.

What we feel affects how we think and act. So, to change how we think and act, change the emotion. Louise knew that!

What we do affects how we feel and think. So, to change how we feel and think, change what you're doing. Mammy knew that!

So, we have learned that we can change how we feel, how we think and what we do. We can set our own vibrations and intentions for the day. We can be intentional with our energy and our time. We have one life to live. We don't need to be caught up in the story of our lives or attach ourselves to the emotion of it all.

The body is a wonderful tool for us. It keeps the score and holds all the answers. When we stop and listen to our intuition, our inner knowing, our inner voice, our higher self … call it what you will … there is an innate wisdom, and it knows what is going on. We just have to listen. Our emotions are supposed to be our ruling guide. We have no need to fear them. Allow them and let them be. Listen to the messages behind them; *what is the body trying to tell us?* Who would have thought shoulder pain was caused by trapped grief? What can *you* acknowledge, process and release today? And what would you like it to be replaced with? What are you choosing for yourself?

Looking to the future

As the mother of a 4-year-old boy, I am proud and grateful for the journey I've been on; for all the lessons and experiences I've had, for all the tools I've learned. I will use and continue to share them with as many people as I can.

The most important person I enjoy sharing these tools with, is my son Francis.

I want him to have all the tools at his disposal; to understand his own emotions, to have a name for what that bubble of energy in his body is, to listen to his emotions, and to release them and let them go too. I want him to grow up knowing he is loved, valued, adored, and no emotion he feels is too big or too small. He will have lots of tools for processing his emotions and whatever life throws his way. I want him to make healthy choices for himself, his family and how he chooses to show up in the world with a family that loves him. And I hope he remembers what his mammy taught him.

MAIREAD MCDONALD

M y name is Mairead McDonald and I was born and raised on the Fermanagh Monaghan Cavan border in Ireland. I grew up in a busy tight knit family of 9 children, at the end of the Troubles. We spent lots of time, not always by choice… in the farm and on the bog. We got to know lots of people in the community through our parents and their interests. The outdoors was part of our childhood. Nurturing wellbeing, self-care and taking personal responsibility is very important to me and as you will read, is something I learned from my mum in my teenage years.

I am mum myself to a 4-year-old boy who I adore watching learn and develop and am constantly amazed at the speed of his growth. I work as a Social Care Worker with children in care and am proud to be part of a very proactive team, with excellent support, doing our best to provide the children in our care with all the support, understanding, guidance and direction they need.

I work as a Wellness Coach with groups of parents in the community under Wellness From Within. I facilitate six-week programs for people to learn a variety of tools for self-care, self-regulation, introspection and self-love and acceptance. Parents are nurtured throughout the sessions with little gifts and support, from each other and from me, and I share many tools and experiences I have learned over the years. These are tools for regulation, validation of your own experience and connecting to your own inner wisdom and guidance. I provide signposts in the community for anyone needing further support and I love connecting people with other therapists and practitioners in the area.

I am a proud Usui Reiki Master. I channel healing reiki energy, in person or over a distance. The healing power of reiki is beautiful, and people don't need to relive their trauma or experience, the reiki does the healing.

I really enjoy and feel great value in incorporating wellness practices into my own everyday life. I will often meditate, journal and move in the mornings, I am often found outside standing barefoot on the grass in the healing power of nature. DoTerra essential oils are my go-to support for emotional wellbeing and I use these almost daily. They are very ethically sourced, and each bottle contains 100% pure oil, they support on a cellular level, and there is literally an oil for everything. From scarring to teething, anxiety to sleep, digestion to compassion, cleaning and hand-creams. They are the go-to in our house and are regularly diffused or applied to the soles of our feet. My son is congested this week and I've been using a vapour stick to relieve the blockage from his airways, it's working wonders!

I also enjoy getting out into nature, to waterfalls, beaches, nice drives. I enjoy movement of many kinds such as yoga, swimming, walks, the gym again recently and jiving. I feel well when I eat well, although I enjoy regular treats as well, I've a bit of a sweet tooth. I gain great enjoyment and benefit from connecting with like-minded people, both personally and professionally.

The true goal is to provide parents with all the wellbeing tools for supporting themselves and sharing with their families. Wouldn't it be wonderful for our children to be able to label and express how they feel and have valuable tools for self-care to manage their own wellbeing, whatever life offers them.

Mairead's Facebook is www.facebook.com/wellnessfromwithin2021

NO MAN, NO HOUSE, NO MONEY
ELISABETH GABAUER

No man, no house, no money … but happy

My journey starts years ago when I had a wake-up call. I was sitting in my daily morning-meditation when suddenly something really weird happened inside of my body. I would say I was set on fire. It got so hot inside my body that I thought my whole body burnt. The heat all over my skin was nearly unbearable.

First of all, I thought about the room temperature but then I realized that all the heat came from inside my body. I was able to pinpoint exactly, where it came from my heart. Inside my chest was no longer a "normal heart" it was a big fireball.

I started sweating, but without sweat. I know it sounds crazy but hang in there it gets even crazier. I opened my eyes and I saw that my skin became completely red, like when I was in a sauna too long. The heat was really unendurable, so I thought about ending the meditation.

But I couldn`t move my body. Although I felt this tremendous heat all over my body coming from the center of my chest, I felt frozen in my meditation posture. I told myself: "Maybe this is a dream" I opened my eyes again and it was definitely clear that it wasn`t a dream, everything was real. While I was checking the situation, I heard a very loud voice saying: "You are not meant to be here"

Wow. That voice hit me.

After a while I was able to stand up. I opened the door to my garden to let fresh air in. I was standing, looking at my beautiful backyard and my lovely house and I still heard that voice saying "You are not meant to be here" I was confused

I love meditation, because meditation helps me to observe all my thoughts and feelings and dive into a deeper place of being. I call this deeper place of being my essence. When the outside overwhelms me, I always go to this silent place to regulate myself. This morning I got to a very deep place of silence and suddenly all these weird things happened to me.

I had this voice in my ears for days and I stopped meditating for weeks, which was very unusual for me. I was afraid of what was going on.

During this time, I did a lot of research work about body experiences in meditation. I found out that such experiences are happening all the time. I also read a few articles from neuroscientists that explained those heat experiences neurophysiologically, that really calmed me down. My mind was satisfied.

So I started meditating again. I sat down and very soon the voice was here again. This time I could feel the truth in it. Yes, it was true it was time for a change. I could feel a long time before that something was going on in my life. I didn't know what kind of change exactly, but I had this gut feeling long before. And I knew already that this house, this place was a stopover, I was not meant to settle down for a long time. What I didn't realize at the time was, that it was not only about my house or the town I lived in, it was about my whole life.

The next few days I dove deep into myself. I looked at my life very honestly. I truly observed my state of being and what I found out was that I was living a life based on shame, fear, fights and feelings of not being good enough. My life was based on the expectations of others, or rather what I believed what others expected on me. Slowly the curtain fell, the veil lifted.

Normally when I was unsatisfied with something I sat down with myself and figured out what I had to change. And sometimes I had this feeling inside myself that I call a "small wake up". This is the moment when you become aware of something, when you see connections more clearly and you realize that you have to do something different in your life. Sometimes it is only a reframe of some thoughts or a small daily habit and sometimes it's a huge thing. Maybe you know this feeling, this gut feeling that tells you if something is good or bad for you. You can also call it intuition or awareness.

I always had good access to my intuition, to my essence and more or less I trusted this inner guidance. As you read this chapter, I am sure you know what I mean. Sometimes you know this inner truth and it can be very scary to fully trust and follows this inner knowing. Often this means giving up something safe and creating something new. I've already had this kind of changes in my life. There were a lot of transformations before. Relationships ended or started, some moves from one town to another, changes in my business or in friendships but this time I could feel it was not only about something it was about everything.

These days of meditating, this kind of retreat going deep into myself, showed me that most of the time I have lived a life that didn't correspond with my true authentic self but to the values of a more or less sick society and standards of other people. A big amount of my lifetime I was worrying how others felt about me instead of how I felt. I met the demands of other people and the society in which I lived. I reached the goal on the outside but deep down on the inside I was sad and lonely. Furthermore, it was only possible to maintain this life with great effort. I felt daily stressed to reach all this unspoken goals of my sick reality, I was living in. If you want to fit in you have a lot of rules which your life depends on. This patriarchal system holds us women small with all of this rules. You have to look pretty, no matter what. You have to be well organized all the time, to have your life under control is your daily task. You have to be the perfect mother, wife, housewife and on top your business should be at least a multifigured one. What the f....

To be focused on all these rules doesn't allow you to feel the life in you. Literally, you don't have time for your life! I was obsessed doing everything right without knowing what was right. That frustrated me and made me tired.

Of course, I was tired and frustrated, because it always takes a huge amount of energy to be someone else, to play a role and to reach goals that are meaningless in itself. It's not natural to live life this way. Human beings are not meant to live their lives that way.

As I dived deep into this process, and started meditating again, I realized that there wasn't any joy in my life anymore. I lost the love for life. My life was about completing daily tasks. No joy, no fun, only problems to resolve. It was sad.

As I realized this, I also realized the meaning of the sentence "You are not meant to be here"

It was not about the house, It was about my life generally.

"This life wasn't meant to be my life! My life was meant to be joyful, to be full of energy. I was meant to live a high energetically life, a life full of love and happiness"

I realized that I was at the wrong place at the wrong time.

Wow. That hit me again.

What was wrong with my life?

I had two healthy and absolutely wonderful children, a house, a nice man and also a profitable business. Why would I want to change that?

In first place it wasn't about those things to change because of first sight they were all good. It was about the recognition that I was a fake. I wasn't the woman I was meant to be. What do I mean with that? I mean that my life was built based on a lot of subconscious believes Beliefs how life should be, how I should be and not based on my authentic self. I was playing a role and I was so identified with that role that I believed it was me.

I had this core thought, that I had to take care of everybody's emotional state more than mine. Most of the time I lived my life to behave like others want me to behave, so that they could stay in their comfort zone. I noticed that I built my life absolutely on pleasing other people. I always thought about the others first. "What can I do to make them feel comfortable and happy?" This question ran my life. Do not get me wrong. This question, is a very important question, especially if you are a mother and you have to take care of your children but not generally in life. You do not have to take care of everyone.

Of course, I learned this behavioral pattern in my childhood because of living with a mother who was suffering from depression and was addicted to psychotropic drugs. Later in life she committed suicide because of her ongoing suffering. Growing up in this environment didn't give me any space to express my needs and wishes. I didn't even feel them.

Sadly, my mother had a lot of traumas stored in her body. Her whole life she had to play a role and to be able to play this role she needed to suppress all her feelings and needs. Alcohol and antidepressants are very helpful in doing so. She always tried to function in her role. She was a people pleaser par excellence, the only boundary she set in her life was herself -imposed death.

As a child I learned to take care of my parent's emotional state and put my needs away. It was a helpful behavior at this time but now as a mature woman it wasn't necessary anymore and besides I got myself in troubles with that, because I ignored my needs and my inner truth. My soul already cried and my body suffered.

Thank goodness, I didn't use alcohol or drugs for it. I used my perfectionism and my behavior patterns to suppress my true self. My behavior was the behavior of the "nice girl". This was my unhealthy role that I based my life on.

I only felt safe when everybody around me was happy and regulated but that's an impossible task. You can't always live your life in a way that everybody around you is satisfied. I had to fail at this goal. But every time I "failed", I felt like a big failure and not being enough. The believe of never being enough, never doing enough, never having enough was my underlying believe that ran my life. And this core belief, let me live in lack although I had everything.

What I learned about myself on this journey was that I had to immediately stop to live my life this way and to become my authentic self. I wanted to get to know my true self and to become who I really was in the depth of my soul.

The nice girl had to die so that the woman I was meant to be could come alive

After realizing that I had forgotten myself by looking at what others needed or wanted and deciding to build my life around my authentic self, everything changed, really everything. No stone was left unturned.

I started working on my people pleasing patterns, I worked on shame, blame and grief and I worked out how to express myself in a loving and respectful way. I learned to surround myself with people who treated me respectfully and to say no to people who don't. I challenged myself to become so brave, that I was able to make decisions based on my inner truth, even if others didn't agree with them.

I really had to break the habits of my old self. It was absolutely clear to me, that this old identity had built my life, the life "I am not meant to live". So, if I lost my identity, I had to lose my life too. And this was exactly what happened to me.

My old life had totally fallen apart and I dove deep into the unknown to find myself.

Little by little I reclaimed my true self and became rooted in my essence.

Life pushed me through all my limiting believes, all my shame and worthlessness. I had to feel everything I tried my whole life to avoid. It showed me with every upcoming problem on the outside more about my strength and my power at the inside. Life initiated me. Life helped me to reclaim my worth and to find my inner truth. At this time, I lost my house, all my money, my business, most of my friends and my marriage. I ended up with nothing on the outside but with everything on the inside. This was the opportunity for me building my life based on my authentic self, based on my truth.

Life has given me the chance to start over again.

Now I deeply believe in life. Like a child I'll always follow the energy. I am deeply interested in what makes my heart jump joyfully and what increases the energy in my system. Sometimes it's a thought or an inspiring book or a joyful conversation. If there is joy in it, I follow it. Maybe you have experienced this too, you have a thought about the possibility of a project and suddenly you have all the energy available for it. Or you are tired and suddenly only one word in a conversation puts your energy up into a higher level and you start to follow it with your focus. This is what I mean with I follow the energy. I always compare this state of "knowing what is right" to the state of falling in love. If you know someone or something is right for you, you fall in love with it. When you are in love you suddenly have a lot more energy, life is more beautiful and at ease. Everything tastes and smells better and you yourself are happier. To me, it's some kind of falling in love with life itself.

To be connected with the life inside myself it's an ongoing love story to me.

Now I deeply enjoy myself and all the beautiful things life offers me. To let go of the role of the nice girl saved my life and made me much more kind to myself and also to all the people around me. To know my worth and to be guided by my inner truth made me unstoppable.

The journey to my authentic self is the most amazing thing I have experienced in my life.

The most beautiful trip I ever got on.

ELISABETH GABAUER

*"*I**f a woman knows her worth and is guided by her inner truth, she is unstoppable"

Elisabeth Gabauer is a body and soul therapist in Austria, located near Vienna. Her working tools are osteopathy, coaching, psychosociology and Naikan. She has also been working as a birth doula for seventeen years.

Due to her family history, she was interested in psychotherapy and body therapy from a very early age. She has been practicing yoga and meditation ever since the age of sixteen, always fascinated by the connection between body and mind. The suffering of women in her family, especially the suffering and illness of her mother, brought her to the profession of therapy.

First of all osteopathy, because she loves the voice of the body. Elisabeth says, 'Even if you can't speak for yourself, your body will do it for you.'

With the beginning of her therapeutic career, a great interest in spirituality came into her life. This curiosity led her to practicing Buddhist meditation, which is her daily basis of life and this preoccupation with meditation brought her to Naikan. Naikan is her big love and for her the best way of bringing women closer to their essence. Naikan is a combination of Japanese psychotherapy and meditation. In a ten-day retreat you will be confronted with the three essential questions of life and thus find your way back to your inner self. You can read her story about Naikan in the book "*Naikan - Eintauchen ins Sein*".

Working as a birth doula opened up the world of women in sisterhood to her. Elisabeth says, 'During a birth you are very close to the source of life and the power of femininity.' Her work with women is the work of her heart.

In Austria she gave birth to the 'Weiberkraft Movement', now patented. This movement is a regular gathering of women in sisterhood to develop and support each other. She is also the founder of a podcast called *Frauencouch,* which gives women the possibility to tell their stories and empower others. Moreover she accompanies women for twelve months in their personal development in her program "The Female Alchemy".

She is currently teaching Naikan based life and social counseling with her Naikan mentor, Yoshin Franz Ritter, at the Naikan-Institut and she teaches a new way of osteopathy based on spirituality. She has named this training SoulTouch.

She also did a lot of training in systemic family therapy and trauma therapy. She is currently doing her master's degree at the Sigmund Freud University in Vienna. It's all about women's needs in a toxic patriarchal society.

She calls herself 'the beloved of life' because she knows that everything in life that happens to you happens for you. It is just life's attempt to bring you to your essence. Sometimes life gets hard and narrow only to give birth to a better version of yourself.

Who do you want to be? How do you want to live and feel? New choices give you new possibilities.

Her mission is to support women to overcome all their limiting believes and circumstances to reconnect with their wonderful essence, to live a vibrant, joyful and pleased life.

Elisabeth's website is www.elisabethgabauer.at

UNLEASHING MY INNER HEALING FORCES
ELAINE CURRY

THE POWER OF HEALING FROM WITHIN

My lifelong passion has always been helping those living and suffering with psoriasis. This journey began when I was diagnosed with this debilitating skin disease at the age of fifteen. At the onset, my arms had just a few mild spots. However, as the years went by, these spots transformed into larger, angry red patches that began to cover my body and consume my life with suffering and war with my body for ten years.

It all started after I had strep throat and glandular fever in my teens, affecting my school studies for six months in the middle of my GCSE year and pausing my athletic passions of netball, cross-country and hockey. Losing nearly two stone and recovering to fight back better was the first health scare I experienced in my young life.

The doctor prescribed steroids and coal tar creams, and little did I know that this would be the start of a long and gruelling battle with psoriasis. I reluctantly slathered on these sticky, foul-smelling creams, unaware of the potential side effects they carried. When I eventually stopped using them, the condition returned even worse. Over time, psoriasis didn't spare any part of my body, spreading to my scalp, neck, back, chest and legs. At its peak, 80% of my body was covered in psoriasis and I was hospitalised many times. But today, an occasional spot on my arm is a mere reminder of the past, and I've learned how to control it drug-free.

I often wish I had the knowledge I possess now when I was first diagnosed. It could have saved me years of suffering in silence. If you are reading this and living with psoriasis, know you are not alone. Have faith that you can help with diet and lifestyle changes, just as I did.

Psoriasis is a relentless, chronic condition that goes deeper than the skin. During my worst times, I battled depression and even contemplated suicide. Psoriasis dominated my life for ten years as I explored various treatment options, consuming my time searching for a cure. However, I realised that conventional medication offered only short-term relief and brought too many side effects. That's when I embarked on my journey to find a better solution of diet and lifestyle changes.

For years, psoriasis controlled me, but from the age of twenty-five, I was connected to a naturopath and learned how to control it. I am determined to share the knowledge and experience I have gained over the years so that others can reclaim their lives too. My success in holistically treating psoriasis is documented in my book to share widely my transformation story, and my message is clear: *Control Your Psoriasis Don't Let It Control You.*

My clear skin results are the product of adopting a holistic approach to healthy skin. This approach combines the wisdom of naturopathic and holistic treatments with modern diagnostic tools, emphasising the body's innate ability to heal itself. My unwavering commitment to this belief has enabled me to manage, control and ultimately clear my psoriasis.

Thanks to three decades of research, trial and error, and the personal experience of living with this chronic skin condition, I take pride in achieving clear skin within weeks after any flare-up during very stressful times.

Though a cure for psoriasis has not been found, lifestyle changes and effective skin care management can provide patients with optimal control. Here are some quick tips:

1. Maintain good health habits, adopt an alkaline diet.
2. Quit smoking and limit unwanted chemicals in your body.
3. Avoid alcohol and any foods that increase inflammation.
4. Manage stress and adapt good self-care.
5. Avoid medications that worsen psoriasis.
6. Maintain good skin care, and keep hydrated.
7. Avoid throat and gut infections and support your immunity.
8. Treat the skin disease promptly, from the inside out.
9. Learn to live with psoriasis and adapt a new way of living for an optimised living.

I now provide a twelve-week 'Clear My Psoriasis' support program, empowering individuals to make transformative changes and detoxify their bodies. Through personalised coaching and unwavering support, I assist clients in managing their psoriasis. Remember, while there may not be permanent cures for diseases or health conditions, you can regain control and live a fulfilling life. The right intervention can stop long-term suffering.

RESILIENCE IN THE RUBBLE – THRIVING DURING RELATIONSHIP BREAK-UPS

As a young girl with dreams of building a loving family, I believed that my life would follow the same path as my parents, who had a relationship built on love, respect and support. But as I ventured into young adulthood, my dreams seemed to crumble, and I found myself trapped in abusive, controlling and unhealthy relationships.

Growing up, I had never been exposed to domestic violence. My father was a loving and supportive figure. So, when the first signs of abuse crept into my life, I didn't recognise them for what they were.

The abuse began slowly, with nipping, verbal insults, to physical and emotional torment. It escalated to a point where I felt like I was sleeping with the enemy, trapped in a place called home that should have been nurturing and safe but had turned into a prison. The film *Sleeping With the Enemy*, featuring Julia Roberts, became a beacon of hope for me, showcasing the possibility of breaking free from a controlling, abusive partner. In moments of torment, I yearned for that freedom with a glimmer of hope.

Years of enduring abuse took a toll on my self-esteem with suicidal thoughts. I learned that a person meant to be your protector could use physical power to diminish your self-worth, leaving you feeling lost and disempowered. Living with an abusive partner was living in perpetual fear, a constant cycle of danger, manipulation and control.

It's essential to recognise that conflict, behaviour changes and disagreements are normal in any relationship. Men and women think and act differently, and their needs and desires may not always align. People have different personalities, strengths and weaknesses. But in a healthy relationship, partners should be free to express their opinions, values and dreams without hostility.

Control, however, can lead to isolation from friends and family, verbal abuse, judgement and disapproval of choices, ultimately robbing the controlled partner of their identity. Leaving such a relationship can be challenging, especially for those financially dependent on their abusers.

When you are vulnerable to control, you become disconnected from yourself, conforming to your partner's ideals and standards. This pattern of control can strip away your sense of self, leaving you feeling lost and not functional and scared of the unknown.

In toxic relationships, conflicts become never-ending, with drama, doubts and fear replacing resolutions. Boundaries are blurred, lies become the norm and trust and communication break down. Leaving such relationships has been essential for my mental health and wellbeing long-term. Battling a chronic skin condition was not going to be easy while also enduring a toxic relationship.

One way I help others address conflict in a relationship is to set aside time for open communication. Taking time to discuss feelings and concerns can help improve the quality of a relationship. Talk about various aspects of life, such as mindset, health, relationships, work, spirituality and lifestyle changes. Be honest, empathetic and kind in your discussions.

When conflict escalates into domestic violence, it's crucial to say NO. I realised that I had forgotten who I truly was deep in toxic relationships, isolating myself from friends and family out of embarrassment or fear. But I knew deep down I deserved better, even when my partner tried to destroy my identity and character with lies, manipulation and deceit. Knowing your self-worth and holding a deep value for who you really are gives you strength.

Coping with abuse presents a distinct challenge compared to managing everyday conflicts. It is imperative that no-one ever feels unsafe within the sanctuary of their own home. Each day, I steadfastly reminded myself that I deserved a loving and healthier life, all the while concealing my pain behind a reassuring smile for the sake of my daughter, who remained my unwavering source of hope and sunshine amid the gloomy days.

Throughout my most trying times, I managed to journal, read books, devised weekly routines, set goals, prioritise self-care and ensure I nourished my body by preparing food plans. My determination to function at my best was unwavering, and I channelled my passion into creating charitable initiatives and supporting those who were less fortunate. The joy I derived from these endeavours significantly eased my transitions.

Escaping the clutches of an abusive partner or an unhealthy relationship is a lengthy and challenging path. It involves tackling feelings of loss, mourning the potential that was never realised, releasing the past and embarking on the journey of creating a new life, all of which require time and the support of a caring network. This journey may be marked by the emergence of post-traumatic stress but also it was a period of post-traumatic growth, with a sense of invaluable liberation and empowerment. I discovered the reservoir of inner strength within me and the unwavering faith with a determination to distance myself from future conflicts and establish healthy boundaries. This energised me to foster self-respect, nurture my personal and professional growth and cultivate a steadfast faith in God, ultimately placing my trust in the process of healing and renewal.

Never let your relationships define you. Instead, let them empower you to say no to what you don't deserve and design a better, more peaceful life nourishing life. Life is full of choices, and the freedom to make them can lead to a happier, more fulfilling, joyful existence.

EMBRACING THE CHANGE – DISCOVERING JOY IN MENOPAUSE

Navigating the uncharted waters of menopause was a journey I reluctantly embarked on in my forties, coming to the end of my procreation years. I had been tiptoeing around the subject, blissfully unaware of the impending hormone roller-coaster. In my mind, the absence of night sweats meant I had nothing to worry about just yet. Little did I know that perimenopause was a maze of thirty-plus symptoms affecting my body, mind and emotions, as I navigated my midlife years.

It all started in my early forties, as my once-vibrant health started to decrease. I found myself making more frequent trips to the GP, experiencing intense shoulder stiffness and battling new-found fatigue. Mental health changes also crept in, with heightened anxiety and uncharacteristic emotional lows. I even had moments of sheer panic, fearing I had cancer due to lumpy breasts. It took two long years of uncertainty to connect the dots and attribute these symptoms to perimenopause.

At age forty-six, an accidental TV appearance by Davina McCall served as a wake-up call. I felt an undeniable urge to pause my life and understand what was happening to me. The journey ahead was isolating and frightening, with a visit to a Framer Health Clinic in Belfast offering me the first glimpse of my hormonal reality. The naturopath informed me I was premenopausal, though the significance eluded me until two years later when I realised I was in the depth of perimenopause.

As I reached age forty-seven, my once-predictable periods became irregular, and I found myself perpetually uncomfortable. Irritability seeped into my personal and professional relationships, and I could hardly recognise myself. I was consumed by bouts of low tolerance, unrelenting tiredness and waves of low moods. My coping mechanism was disconnecting from the world and taking a deep pause.

At the age of forty-eight, hot flushes emerged, my skin itched incessantly and tears flowed freely with an overwhelming sense of increased anxiety. I had been living life in high gear for years, but now I yearned for the serenity of gear two and wanted to hit the pause button. My life was spiralling, and I feared losing my grip on reality. In March 2023, I finally admitted to my struggle and sought the guidance of a menopause coach, Maria, as my symptoms intensified at age forty-eight.

Navigating perimenopause was far from straightforward. My symptoms included severe sleep disturbances, low energy, headaches, dizziness and tearfulness. I'd find myself crying for hours, unable to identify the cause. The relentless exhaustion and plummeting confidence left me in a constant state of unease. My behaviour became erratic, characterised by over-shopping, overthinking and overanalysing.

The most harrowing symptom was the lack of sleep, compounded by anxiety, headaches and dizziness. Even driving became a nerve-wracking ordeal. My enlightenment came through an online menopause course that revealed I was not alone in my ordeal.

During my sleepless nights, I would search for remedies, amassing a small fortune in menopause products. During these sleepless nights, I stumbled upon Maria, my menopause coach, who guided me through the chaos.

It wasn't easy to secure a doctor's appointment, and I had to shed the facade of being 'fine'. As a coach, it was especially challenging to admit that I, too, needed help.

Menopause, a natural part of ageing, impacts women differently. Some embrace change, while others struggle with emerging symptoms. Understanding hormones, embracing menopause and acknowledging individual symptoms are keys to navigating this transition, as well as monitoring insulin, cortisol and oxytocin levels.

To find joy in menopause, I have devised ten essential tips:

1. Listen to your body: Understand your top three symptoms, get blood tests and seek a second opinion.
2. Pause and reflect: Prioritise an intentional wellness self-assessment and look at where you can change your habits.
3. Engage and talk: Share your experiences with others, creating a supportive community.
4. Remember your uniqueness: Individual factors like relationships, family and stress levels significantly influence your experience.
5. Be creative: Journal your emotions, explore new interests and embrace the emerging you – find joy in new interests.
6. Lower stress: Identify and eliminate stress triggers to manage cortisol levels.
7. Eat well to age well: Prioritise a healthy diet to ease symptoms and boost your energy, nourish the body and balance blood sugar levels.
8. Find your joy: Discover activities that bring you happiness, whether it's swimming, art, dance or something new.
9. Be kind to yourself: Practice self-compassion and prioritise self-care.
10. Invest in yourself: Seek resources, join support groups and consider one-on-one coaching.

Drawing from personal experience, I'm dedicated to empowering women in hormone mastery and personalised wellness plans. If you are navigating the turbulent journey of menopause, remember that understanding your body, embracing the process and acknowledging your individual experience can lead to optimal health. Through this transition, we can become a better, stronger version of ourselves with new-found joy.

Our strength is tested in adversity, revealing our capabilities and nurturing a passion for empathetic support. Choosing bravery, deep love and unwavering determination makes us unstoppable forces. Life is an adventurous journey where our choices define the joy of each new day. I wish my life to symbolise relentless faith, boundless hope and the healing power of love and nourishing foods. Together, with caring companions, we enhance lives. Our stories are ongoing, and future chapters will be filled with courage, love and unstoppable spirits. We are born to overcome, and each sunrise offers a fresh day in the epic adventure of our lives, where we paint the beauty of our dreams.

ELAINE CURRY

I'm Elaine, an ageing well coach and consultant, specialising in personal and professional development. My career path has led me through the fascinating fields of psychology, NLP, strategic planning and development. On my journey, I have unearthed my true passion for coaching, mentoring, training and consultancy – *transforming lives and building communities.*

My mission is to create positive transformations, empower individuals and encourage communities to thrive, serving as a guiding light and inspiration on their life or professional journeys.

For twenty-five years, I have immersed myself in the world of health improvement and program development, aimed at helping people live their lives to the fullest and creating age-friendly communities. My life's path has been deeply rooted in the heart of Northern Ireland, where I've collaborated with charities and government departments to make a meaningful impact on countless lives.

My journey and passion have been defined by three significant challenges. Firstly, I battled psoriasis, a persistent chronic skin condition, which first appeared when I was just age fifteen. Through years of research and experimentation, I cracked the code for managing psoriasis naturally. My success isn't just a personal victory but a ray of hope for others with similar inflammatory skin conditions.

Secondly, I endured heart-wrenching relationship break-ups that altered my mental and physical health but also instilled in me a profound determination and a new sense of identity and purpose. They taught me invaluable lessons in self-esteem, resilience, empathy and managing my own wellbeing. These lessons now help me to guide those seeking to heal their broken hearts and develop healthier, more fulfilling relationships.

Lastly, I navigated the turbulent menopausal hormone roller-coaster in my forties. With unwavering determination and specialised support, I emerged from this experience with a new-found mission to support other women on their own menopausal journeys.

I aim to share my story of transformation, resilience and unwavering dedication to my mission. I'm committed to helping individuals and communities develop personal and professional plans, offering one-on-one support and group programs to ensure people live well and age well. I'm also a great advocate for those dealing with skin issues, menopause care, holding wellness events, deep connected to community and ageing well programs.

Over the past fifteen years, I've developed a range of programs that empower people to achieve optimal health and wellness. My focus includes assisting individuals in managing life transitions, better sleep, stress management, emotional control, improving relationships, over-coming break-ups, enhancing self-care routines, increasing energy, improving gut health and skin health, finding their life purpose and transitioning careers.

In a world that constantly challenges us, I want to stand as a beacon of hope, offering support, guidance and knowledge to help individuals and communities flourish. My journey may have been marked by obstacles, but it is through overcoming these challenges that I've found my true purpose: to inspire and empower others to lead healthier, more fulfilling lives.

Elaine's website is www.elainecurrycoaching.com

I NEVER WANT TO SAY, 'I WISH I'D DONE THAT,' I WANT TO SAY, 'I CAN'T BELIEVE I DID THAT!'

JOANNE COLELY

The castle knew we were coming well before we did. It had already chosen us. It was manifested, all it had to do was wait. A silent witness to our imminent arrival, an ethereal manifestation patiently waiting on our arrival.

As the taxi driver traversed the weathered, uneven path, I caught a glimpse of the majestic, grandiose, looming castle unfolding before me.

The sun had dipped below the horizon, casting a warm glow upon the ancient structure. The dark silhouettes of the tall trees reached out like long dark spindley fingers against the darkening violet coloured sky and the woods gave way almost as if nature itself was pointing to the ancient, majestic yet mysterious building.

As we drew closer, I caught my breath. In a small clearing, deer grazed and a regal stag stood proudly poised, locking eyes with me staring in my direction. It's as if time stood still for just a moment as we exchanged a long look. A shared moment of connection. He then turned his head thoughtfully to the side and then led his herd from the clearing deeper into the woods as the taxi drew closer to the castle.

They had nothing in common, yet they were drawn together.

I knew before I left that it would be a group of strong women. A knowing, well before my departure that this would comprise a collective of formidable women.

My eyes widened as I took in the opulence of the room, the strong earthy woody smell of the candles, the musk of the scattered antiques and ancient tapestries hanging about the dark wood lining the walls. The roar of the fireplace and the tinkling of crystal glasses as the butler and maid gracefully bustled about serving the fine food on their best China.

They had nothing in common and yet here we were from every corner of the world, diverse backgrounds yet brought together for a purpose I won't know about for years to come. Amidst the opulent surrounding, the enchantment of the castle lingered, a mystical force weaving its magic. A smile tugged at the corner of my mouth as the sparkling eyes and playful smiles of the cheeky women sitting nearby, hinted at a life-long connection. It was as if destiny itself had orchestrated our meeting in this magical abode.

I can't explain it but there was real magic in this castle.

A curtain of red hair and the brightest blue eyes I've ever seen flashed before me as she walked powerfully yet purposelessly into the room. A commanding presence, I had just prior stood nervously with the painting I had worked on for months, yet she set me immediately at ease with her warm smile. Her face lit up as she stopped abruptly staring at the image looking back at her. Her eyes darted to me as she spoke. "So! Do you think I look at all like the photo I sent you in order to paint this?" She paused, her eyes sparkling mischievously yet with a happy smile on her face. "I feel like I have captured your inner strength and certainly your eyes and your spark," I replied eyes widening as I marvelled that here I was having a chat with the Duchess of York Sarah Ferguson in a castle, miles away from my home in Australia. This is a moment in my life I will never forget.

Later that evening, the gala at the castle became a sea of sequins, twinkling candlelight, the sound of laughter and the champagne was flowing into the beautiful crystal glasses. Suddenly, a new woman entered the room. Her very presence immediately lit up the room with her sparkling irish smiling eyes and wide grin, however there was something more. A deep wisdom and a charm of older times well before these. It was as if she had lived many lifetimes before this. As her eyes locked with mine across the room I felt a deeper connection as if we had known each other long before this.

This connection led me to now be sitting on the other side of the world in Perth Western Australia. As I sit with the sparkling blue ocean beckoning me from the cafe where I now sit and where I love to create my best ideas, I close my eyes and feel the words wash over me. So many amazing twists and turns, how on earth did my life go in the incredible direction that it did and still continues to do? How on earth did I get to a castle in Europe and meet the Duchess of York? How did I turn my life around when only a few short years ago, I fell to my knees in despair thinking my life had no purpose or meaning? One thing that kept me going. I have come from a strong line of women before me and I have two daughters who I need to teach to keep going and make the impossible possible.

I spent 22 years working in corporate. I was great at it, but every day when my alarm would go off I had a feeling of dread. I knew I needed to dramatically change my life in order to bring change. I had to trust that I needed to listen to my heart more often. We are all born with gifts. Once you discover them, you must give them away. Never let your gifts stop with you.

This is also where I discovered the power of mindset.

Years ago, I was told that I was no good at painting and so I believed it. I 'chose' to believe it so for 10 years I didn't paint. But one day I saw a post on facebook that was a quote that said "One day I woke up and decided that I didn't want to feel like this anymore. So I changed." I loved it so much I made it my cover photo to remind myself that this is what I wanted to do. Back then, I felt like I was in such a dark place that I felt like I was buried, but actually I'd been replanted and the only way from there is up. Who would have thought years later, that I would have gone on to paint the former Prime Minister of Australia among many other celebrities and more recently the Duchess of York Sarah Ferguson raising $200,000 for charities across Australia. I had to change the way I think. Because after all, whether you believe you can or believe you can't, you will be right.

This series of events led me to wanting to help kids to know you're their worth and in turn 'pay it forward.'

I remember the field was freshly cold and the crisp cool wind whipped through my hair. The sun revealed itself as a small chink of light in the far distance and a feeling of dread enveloped me at the thought of the threat of rain. Just weeks earlier I had put it out there into the universe (namely Variety Club Australia and the Magic Coat) where I reached out and asked for a very deserving boy or girl who I could give an uplifting experience to. Within 24 hours I was given a boy and a girl both around 14 with similar bullying circumstances. It felt meant to be and as it turned out it was. I have chills up my arms as I write this. I wanted to surprise both children with an opportunity of a lifetime. I had already organised for the boy Ollie to get a gaming system, however after meeting him, I was concerned he would go further down the rabbit hole. So I also organised for him to be mentored and taught about resilience and they offered a summer camp for him to experience with other kids just like him, to help him feel included, valued and believed in. The girl 'Braydee' I decided that she needed to experience something up in the clouds, so here we were just two weeks later in a field in Northam, hours away in the middle of what felt like at the time 'nowhere'. Liberty Balloon Flights almost cancelled due to the threat of rain but as the sun began to rise and spread rays of light across the beautiful canola covered fields, the clouds started to disappear and we all given the ok to up up and away we go! Braydee's eyes shone with excitement as we all eagerly climbed on and as the balloon gently rose, the land began to disappear below us and turn into a brightly coloured blur of a tapestry of bright yellows and greens. The winter had lingered longer than usual this year, so the bright colours of the canola fields were a kaleidoscope of colour. Braydee broke out in song and entertained us all as we all flew up higher into the sky. Such a magical moment that I know that she will never forget to this day. When we landed I asked her what she thought and she excitedly said that now that she had faced a fear, she now knew that she could do anything and that this was only the beginning. I told her not to be a worrier of what people think, but to be a warrior in life and always continue to step forward. Both kids were then interviewed on a national Foxtel Show called "The Couch' that I am often on to describe their experiences and Braydee was then asked to do work experience there the following year, as she is pursuing her dream of theatre. I believe that we all are given gifts for a reason and that it is our job to help others find theirs too. Random acts of kindness are powerful and I told both kids that out of thousands of children they were chosen for a reason. There are no coincidences. My only thing that I ask in return, is that one day they find a child who is going through a similar thing and that they find a way to lift them up too.

The first experience I ever had with dealing with bullying was when my daughter was in daycare. She complained that a boy and after a few encounters I decided I would approach the daycare. As I walked in to discuss this, my mindset was not only of concern for my daughter, but in the belief that no child is bad. I needed to find out the 'why' little did I know I was about to make a huge difference.

Janet* the owner of the daycares' face did not show an ounce of shock when I told her my concerns. She looked down sheepishly and muttered almost to herself "yes I know exactly the boy your daughter is describing. We have been receiving many complaints about him." I stood there thoughtfully and asked "but what is really going on here with him? Are there any other issues deeper than this do you think? It sounds to me like a big cry for help?" Her sharply drawn eyebrows shot up in surprise and then with relief, as she sat leaning forward staring straight ahead thoughtfully with her hands pressed together, her fingers poking deep into her chin. "His mother was found dead in the shower from a drug overdose late last year just before Christmas. When his father came home and found her like this, he immediately hopped in his car and at great speed drove it head on into a street lamp. The kids were discovered just days later in dirty nappies sitting holding each other in a cot. He had been taking care of his little sister with whatever he could open or reach in the pantry. Their father survived, however he is now a paraplegic. Jacob* and his sister Lucy* are now being raised by their 80 year old grandmother. They were too upset last year to celebrate Christmas, so they just had sandwiches at home with no presents." My hands fluttered to my chest as I blurted "Christmas is just around the corner, what is the grandmother going to do?" Janet* lowered her eyes and tears pricked the corners of her eyes as she whispered, "its all too much for her. She cannot afford fancy gifts and will probably have a quiet day at home again as there is no other family." I put my hand firmly on the counter straightening up and looked her in the eye and said "those kids and grandmother are going to have the BEST Christmas this year, I will make sure of it." And with that I spun on my heel and I knew exactly what I had to do.

I worked in Yellow Pages Perth, a Telstra owned corporate company. I sent out a group email to all staff at the Perth office explaining the situation. I was expecting perhaps a bag or two of some old toys. What I received was something I never in my wildest dreams expected. The kindness of people continues to amaze me to this day. By the end of that week I had filled up an entire storage room at the daycare floor with BRAND NEW toys! Even a pair of ice skates! I even had envelopes filled with money to fill up her fridge with all sorts of Christmas goodies and money for a roast with all the trimmings! The daycare was so surprised they all pitched in and helped wrap each and every present. As there were so many gifts, it was decided to split them over the year for not only Christmas, but also for their birthdays too. This would relieve the stress for the grandmother for the following year. I asked for this all to given to *Doris (the grandmother) anonymously, as it wasn't important to me for her to know who I was. I wanted to restore her faith in humanity and to know that she deserved this. I had heard that *Doris had been very charitable all her life and wasn't very good at receiving. So I wrapped up a small special gift for her and wrote a card and gave it to Janet to give it to her. I sat in my car and as I watched through the window, I saw Janet take Doris's hands. I could see her explaining what was about to happen. Doris's hands flew to her face and she immediately fell back into the chair behind her and began crying as she read my card. She then opened my gift and held up the sparkling glass angel up to the light. My card explained that she is an angel to those children and to hang this glass angel on her tree to remind herself how special she is. I will never forget driving home straight after bawling my eyes out all the way home with pure happiness. I never expected to hear anything about this again, but just a few weeks later, I was delivered a small package to my home from the daycare. My mouth fell open in disbelief as opened up a small photo album. The grandmother had put together an album. The first page had a photo of both kids grinning widely with sparkling eyes into the camera holding a note saying "thank you so much our Christmas angel!" The album was filled with photos of them on their boogie boards, playing on the beach with their buckets and spades, roller skating down the street and even photos of them holding a tin of chocolate Quik with a note saying "We had never tried this before and we LOVE IT!" Such a simple act of kindness gave these kids a memorable happy Christmas, I still think of them today. Those kids would have nearly finished high school now and I often think of them and wonder if I somehow made a difference to their childhood. Perhaps I will never know but I will never forget them.

This taught me to always look from another perspective.

Later that same year my youngest daughter and I had an afternoon nap. Exhausted from my week, it was highly unusual for me to rest during the day, so this was a very rare luxury. I woke not long after to something tickling my face and giggling. As I slowly opened my eyes I was greeted to a room literally filled with broken up pieces of tissues and feathers from an old pillow. I would compare the scene to a winter wonderland and my little daughter had dressed herself in a pink tutu with long stripey multicoloured socks, both arms filled with every bracelet I'm sure she had ever owned and a large hand knitted beanie with a fluffy Pom Pom on top. (To this day she STILL combines the strangest fashion accessories together but somehow pulls it off. This was pre 'Frozen' days otherwise I'm sure she would have been dressed as Elsa.) She had a huge smile on her face as she dramatically threw even more feathers and bits of tissues into the air from a little woven basked, skipping around the room giggling. Now this was my moment. This is where I could choose to tell her off and to clean it up. With a twinkling eyes I chose to jump on the floor immediately and show her how to make snow angels (I have never actually seen snow, but I imagined that this is how you would do it.) Well, her eyes went wide with surprise and delight as she joined me on the floor also making her own snow angel next to me. She is now almost 16 and she still remember this moment to this day. There are always choices on how we choose to look at life.

As children, in the winter we see puddles on the ground as opportunities, yet as adults we see them as obstacles. What happens to our mindset along the way?

The power of your mindset is the key to changing your life. And then you become unstoppable.

JOANNE COLELY

Joanne Colely is dedicated to her craft as a full time professional artist. An International Stevie Award Winner, a cast member of the documentary 'Project Manifest,' she is known throughout the South Pacific as 'the art work' to have in your home. Her astounding achievements since 2020 - 2023 are many and varied. The request to paint the Former Australian Prime Minister Scott Morrison, plus many famous faces which include Daniel Ricciardo, Dr Charlie Teo, Kelly Slater, Ray Meager (Alf from Home and Away), Nat Fyfe, Nick Naitanui among many others. More recently she has been asked to paint the Duchess of York Sarah Ferguson. Painting these politicians and celebrities has raised $200,000 for various charities across Australia.

Her main focus now is painting commissions and selling her collection of works, where her style is extremely diverse. Painting from landscapes to portraits, to a surrealist narrative collection of works and more recently large glass resin pieces with diamond dust and splashes of metallics with mixed media. Some of her works are held by private collectors both nationally and internationally.

Recently she has written, illustrated and published her first children's book 'The Magic Book' and also illustrated the Duchess of York Sarah Ferguson's most recent children's book 'The Forever Tree.'

Please see Joanne Colely's website to view her work and to view her Foxtel interviews to see her latest adventures on www.joannecolely.com. au

THE RIPPLE EFFECT OF
LEAVING A LASTING LEGACY
EMMA LAST

When I say the word legacy what first comes to mind? An amount of money or property left to someone in a will? Or perhaps the long-lasting impact of particular events, actions or collateral that were created in the past or in a person's life?

Well, both of these are accurate but my interest in legacy goes further; in particular its connection to purpose and our overall well-being.

In this chapter, I share the strong link between purpose and legacy and how living with purpose may help you to live longer, along with the nuggets I've learned over the last 20 years in finding my purpose that may help you to feel and become *unstoppable*.

Back in September 2003, my Grandad's funeral was held in a church on the road next to the buildings that had been named after him; the 'Trafford Buildings'. The church was packed with people and many people spoke, even leaders from different religions. It wasn't what you would call a usual funeral.

There were the people he had done charity work with, the people who just knew him for his business, and the people who knew him for his actions and the events he had organised to support the local town and the charities within it. They all wanted to be there and talk about how he had contributed to their lives, what they had learned from him and how he would be missed. In short, his purpose had been serving others.

He touched the lives of so many people. If he'd been there in person, he may not have remembered them all, but they remembered him. They remembered how he brought them together and how he had helped them in some way. He not only left the legacy of the events that still run every year (*well*, apart from the Covid disruption), but he gave them a gift of knowledge, skills or feelings that inspired them to be better people, and to make the world a better place.

I remember sitting with a tissue mopping up my tears thinking, *I want my funeral to be like this. I want people to remember me just like this.* But I couldn't quite put my finger on what I wanted to leave. All I knew was that I wanted service and giving to others to be a part of my life too.

I thought I was on my way and had pretty much nailed it, because at that time I worked for an organisation whose values of trust, service and promotion of all interests, partly gave me this. In reality, we did live by these values, however it felt robotic at times and I sometimes questioned if there might be a deeper connection to a bigger purpose; to something way bigger.

My life got very busy with my career and the birth of our twins, then within three years our third child was born. It wasn't until January 2010 that my view on a deeper purpose started to change.

Our organisation had acquired a large business a few years earlier and over 20 brands had been integrated and rebranded, but I had been asked to work on one of the ones they had left alone until that point.

I was in a small and dingy meeting room in the UK head office of a multinational business. This meeting felt different and looking back I can't even remember the name of the guy in his early 30s, who the meeting was with. However, I definitely do remember what was discussed. My first job was to gain clarity on our vision, mission and proposition to market. I was asking him about the organisation, what he loved about it, where he thought we could improve; to be honest it felt like I had been picked up and dropped in a time warp. This brand had been highly successful, in fact it had been the market leader, but it was on the decline. Although they'd been highly profitable, little investment had gone back into the sustainability of the business. I could see their success was down to them being first in the market and where they had sustained growth, it had been due to their people. Now, these people were not all highly skilled compared to those I had seen before, but they had been there a long time, and they were consistent. They had built strong relationships with their clients, and they loved what they did. As I said earlier, it felt different; the brand felt special. I'd even go as far as saying it was like a precious stone that needed a good polish. This meeting started to change how I viewed the world.

The guy asked, 'have you seen this video by Simon Sinek 'How great leaders inspire action?' We sat and watched it together. To this day, I still remember it … word for word. I only wish I remember all my passwords as well as I remember that video! I listened to the parts about market penetration and then bam, it hit me, 'starting with why - people don't buy what you do they buy why you do it.' That was it. To take these people on this journey, I had to find their why. Why did they love their jobs? Why did they do what they did? What was the bigger cause?

I was curious to know the answer, asking question after question, focus group after focus group. 'The what' was clear; they were a recruitment company and they placed teachers into jobs. 'The how', how they went about getting high quality teaching staff into schools, and *how they could be the best in the market. The Latter* needed work. The systems and processes would need to be updated to make their jobs easier and more failsafe. Many of their staff and teaching staff needed training and coaching so they could thrive. Performance was the easy part for me. I'd been training and coaching all my working life and what I know now, is that

I have what we call in The Change Makers Group (where we use the GC Index), a proclivity for 'Polishing'. I can see the gaps in someone, the ways to improve how someone is feeling or performing, and I can see the gap in the *somethings* - what we need to change, to help them to become more efficient or effective in their work or home life. It's where I quickly create impact.

But I pondered 'the why' over a few weeks. What would be game changing for us both internally and externally? Why were we really doing this? Yes, many would say to make money, and of course we all need to make a living, yet this was much bigger.

Then it came to me. It wasn't about the teachers or the market, it was the ripple effect. If we got 'the why' right it was simple. If we trained everyone on the why and who we were really doing this all for, it would mean all the decisions everyone in the business made on a day-to-day basis would be easy.

And it was the human element of us that connected beautifully to our business purpose. We would be leaving a legacy, and everyone could play their part; some of us even became Governors of schools.

It was about the children, their education, their safety, their happiness, their future. People would want to be part of this big purpose.

And they did.

Watching this play out over the next five years or so was fabulous, even when the market was hard, we felt unstoppable, because our purpose was strong. I was asked to help other brands to find their 'why'. It transformed the culture, and we all knew why we were there and what we needed to do.

In hindsight, I had become so connected with my purpose that I lost some balance in my life. I didn't take the time to check in with myself, and didn't listen to my own needs as I should have along the journey.

But by late 2016 there became a point where this changed. Three brands merged together and amongst all the changes our 'why' started to become unclear. It became more about the what and the how.

I tried to push through the changes, as I had loved a lot of my 19 years, but by late 2017, the decision that I had to leave became clear to me. I sat in our monthly Directors meeting and our MD said, 'how do we get more passion in our people?' That was the day I knew I had to leave. In that moment, I realised she couldn't see that the decisions she had made over the last 12 months had diminished this to something very small, rather than when our 'Why' came first.

I knew how to fix it, but I didn't want to. I couldn't be there anymore. It felt soul-less. It felt robotic. We were back in what felt like no man's land. The land of no purpose. I had become exhausted, burnt out, unhappy and unfulfilled. I was grieving for what we had lost. I felt dead inside. I knew I had to start planning my exit no matter how painful it was going to be. The unstoppable woman was broken.

My Reboot story is for another day, but by early 2018 I had left. Battered and bruised, with my mental health at an all-time low, I had prioritised the business before myself for too long. Now, without purpose, I was left feeling lost. I had to start rebuilding my identity and redefine the mark I wanted to leave in the world, so I absorbed myself in learning and self-development.

I quickly discovered that good mental health is more than the absence of mental illness and that there are two dimensions to mental health; mental health problems, such as anxiety and depression, and positive mental health - our mental wellbeing. Our mental wellbeing is dynamic and can be enhanced by us fulfilling our personal and social goals; the work we do, the people around us, how we achieve a sense of purpose in society. I knew I had to take action to better look after myself, so started looking into wellbeing frameworks, putting some of them into action.

I came across the NHS: *Five steps to wellbeing* which was created by the New Economic Foundation in 2008. To date, I believe it's still one of the best frameworks out there. One of the ways is 'Give' - because giving to others enhances our wellbeing.

I also found research highlighting how giving back can lower blood pressure, reduce cortisol and depression and give our brains the feel-good hormones such as the mood-regulating Serotonin, the sense of pleasure hormone, Dopamine and, as we connect with others, the stress-reducing hormone, Oxytocin.

I quickly found that as I helped others, it boosted my self-esteem and increased my happiness, as well as a lot of other unanticipated benefits.

But my deeper purpose still wasn't clear. I still wanted to help people; I knew that at least.

I started by revisiting my values. I got a big, long list and circled the ones that stood out to me; trust, education, integrity and fairness, to name a few. I wrote down what I stood for and what I stood against. I then reflected on my life experiences, my strengths, skills and passions that shaped who I was to date. I had some beautiful memories that filled me with pride and joy, and some others that made me feel sad or regretful. No matter whether they had been good, bad or painful, these key defining moments had changed the trajectory of my life. They had shaped who I had become and helped me to decide on the way I wanted to live my life. I had forgotten about my thoughts about my Grandad's funeral and my drive to leave a legacy had taken a bit of a detour.

I wanted to find a way to change my pain into purpose. Yes, it would take bravery, but this was a huge learning experience and an opportunity for me to grow, which could help me to leave a legacy I would feel proud of.

I also realised that through events and experiences, I had found my passions, but historically, mine had been too work-focused or were really my children's passions. I had to find passions in more than one area of my life, because if something changed that was out of my control, I would only be losing part of what lit me up not all of it, like I had before.

I moved onto my strengths and skills, and as if by magic, I was introduced to the Japanese concept *Ikigai*, which helps you to find your reason for being by finding the overlap between what you love, what the world needs, what you are good at and what the world will pay for. This helped me to pull this work together, however I knew this time I would be continuing my self-development so I could stay connected to my purpose. I was clear that my purpose was for the long term, not just a short-term goal.

I was reminded of this quote by Mahatma Gandhi - "Be the change you wish to see in the world." I'd seen it before, however this time, I paused and said to myself, *you have the greatest influence on yourself.* I also remembered what one of my mentors had shared with me when I was wanting a promotion: *Act at the level you want to be and it will happen.* I knew that by getting to know myself more deeply, I would be able to shine. I started to be the role model I wanted to see in the world.

I connected with others and shared my learnings. It felt amazing and by giving to others, it really did help my mental wellbeing. I realised I was starting to make the world a better place for others, just by having one conversation at a time. I saw that the little things are sometimes the big things. The book I sent to someone had changed how they viewed themselves. Listening to someone and holding space for them, to help them to empty and process what was going on in their brain, supported them to feel less overwhelmed and able to move forward.

Over time It became clear, I wanted to help workplaces, schools and leaders to view and prioritise their mental health and wellbeing differently, so they could build strong foundations and flourish in their work and life without burning out. This was going to be my legacy.

I thought about my nana who had died about 10 years before my Grandad. We had such special times. She had a love of jewellery; I have a ring and a necklace I treasure. We used to spend hours playing with beads and sparkly objects. She had a love of looking and feeling great, no matter what life throws at you (she had breast cancer). You can put on some clothes and make up that make you feel good and keep going. With a love of books and spirituality; she'd tell me the lost sheep story, as she hooked me out from behind the sofa with a walking stick. She loved self-care, horoscopes, holistic therapies and all things 'woo' including crystals; I loved it all too but had lost contact with it over the years. She also had a love of Minis; I nearly fell out of the car going round a roundabout one day as the door whizzed open. Thankfully all ended well. We still make her 'Passion fruit Ice cream bomb' recipe every Christmas; it's a family tradition.

Just like my Grandad, she brought to life what she loved, what she stood for and against, in the smallest of actions. Both of my grandparents created a ripple effect from the little things they did. They both left me a legacy.

They didn't have to be rich or famous to leave a legacy and neither did I. I had started to Inspire the world within my reach. I wanted to go faster, however I learned that it doesn't always have to be one big thing, it can be a small thing, a small thing that becomes a big thing, or even little things that are really a big thing for someone else.

Edwin Osgood Grover said:

"I am only one,

But still I am one.

I cannot do everything,

But still I can do something;

And because I cannot do everything,

I will not refuse to do the something that I can do."

Whether it was writing a blog, doing a video, being part of 5 book collaborations, setting up my own Human Reboot Podcast, joining or setting up a community, raising money for charity, being a school governor, sharing knowledge, helping hundreds of workplaces and schools, coaching my clients to flourish through my Human Reboot or Tomorrow's Human Programmes, picking up litter or sharing a recipe (notice I haven't said baking or cooking - they definitely didn't go down as one of my strengths). These are some of the small things I've done to leave a bigger legacy.

By taking small sustainable steps towards my legacy, it has helped me to release my power, to become unstoppable, whilst still protecting and enhancing my mental wellbeing.

There is so much going on in the world right now that feels out of our control. It weighs heavy on many of us, however we can all control how we make a difference and what we leave behind. We can all impact others by doing the smallest things, usually through an idea started through a passion, belief, cause or value. And we don't have to wait to do it. By starting an unstoppable ripple effect of hundreds of purposeful positive things that can impact our world, we are leaving a lasting legacy that can make the world a better place...And It may just help you to live a longer, happier and more fulfilled life.

Just like this book, What's the legacy you want to leave?

Poulin, Brown, Dillard, and Smith (2013) examined the association between giving to others and stress reduction
https://pubmed.ncbi.nlm.nih.gov/23327269/

EMMA LAST

E mma Last is a Mental Health Strategist and Speaker. She talks openly about her own burnout after her 19-year leadership career. Through her business Progressive Minds, she supports workplaces, schools and leaders to put in place effective measurable mental health and wellbeing strategies that include training, talks, mentoring and holistic therapies. She is hugely driven to help people to understand both mental health problems and positive mental health, so they can develop the foundations for life, balance their own mental wellbeing, and flourish through her' 'Human Reboot' and 'Tomorrow's Human' Programmes. Three of her courses are Department for Education quality assured. She has twice been an Amazon #1 best-selling author and has spoken on many podcasts, including her own 'Human Reboot'.

Emma's linktree is www.linktr.ee/EmmaLast

PROUD
ALISON ARMSTRONG

On the 20th March 1990 I wrote in my childhood diary

"I am becoming more and more depressed and I feel like my life is over and I will never be happy again. It's awful. I am so sad and I can't stop crying. Suicide would be easy now."

When I wrote this, I was 19 years old and pregnant with twins; a fact which had only been discovered a month earlier. I was already 6 months pregnant when I wrote that, clearly I had reached my capacity to cope and was dealing with deep emotional injury.

Another entry written a few weeks later - 4th April 1990

"I went with my sister shopping after work and bought a few things, we made supper and then unpacked a few boxes. We then made plans for my room and the babies. I wish I was dead."

I now work in Suicide Prevention and have personally trained many people in how to have an *effective suicide intervention* conversation. A conversation that can take a person from isolation to connection and from danger to safety.

What I know now about suicide is that it's difficult to see the signs, at times, impossible. What can appear normal, such as making plans on decorating a bedroom, would never be seen as a sign. But I was acting, playing a part, giving a version of myself everyone else wanted to see. A version that wasn't depressed or full of embarrassment and shame. I may have been making plans on the outside, but it was an act because on the inside, I was making completely different ones.

At the time, I lived in South Africa, and during the 80s being unmarried and pregnant was like going back in time. I was mortified and felt I had let everyone down, especially my father who was so proud of me for being the first in the family to attend university. Having to leave university had such an impact on me. I carried the shame of it for years.

I loved my early formative school years but when I was 10 my family immigrated to South Africa (with a new baby sister), and this changed everything, school wise.

The schooling system was different and corporal punishment was the norm - not for bad behaviour, but for getting things wrong; a sum, a spelling, looking at the teacher the wrong way. I often heard words of … *'you're stupid, why can't you understand?'* The main reason being, was that we were being taught in Afrikaans and I couldn't understand the language, never mind the concepts they were trying to teach, but I was hardly stupid. The worst was watching the boys in my class being canned. It was horrendous. So humiliating for all.

One day, for some reason I don't even remember, I was called to the principal's office and told to go inside. The principal locked the door and told me to pull down my pants and bend over the desk. The principal hit me with a cane. No one had ever hit me this way. I wet myself and he said, *'You're disgusting – Get out.'* I was ten and this was the first time I felt true shame. I sat in class and then on the bus with wet pants, humiliated and ashamed. I never told my parents it had even happened.

Once you feel a strong emotion, the brain has an awful habit of remembering it, and shame typically develops when we look inwardly, with a critical eye, evaluating ourselves harshly from the messages we are given by others. Quite often, this is over things we have little control of. I certainly had no control over wetting my pants, but I carried that feeling of shame that was given to me. Yes given to me.

When I informed the university I was pregnant, I was asked to leave the campus - that very day. Being an unmarried mother meant I had broken the terms and conditions of my bursary. Again, I felt intense shame; shame of letting everyone down and shame for *failing*. It was so intense, it was crippling. I didn't want to go out or see anyone. I worried about who would see me and what they would say. I had brought *shame* upon my family; I was struggling with deep emotional pain.

I went to SAMBA (South Africa Multiple Birth Association) support group, and another mother pregnant with twins told me I would never cope on my own; "it would be better to give them up for adoption," she said.

There wasn't anyone around me listening to me, or asking what I wanted. Decisions were being made for me. I felt lonely, isolated and couldn't talk to anyone about how I was feeling subsequently thinking my life was not worth living.

Those feelings were forced upon me in childhood and again in university, but with some support, I could easily have finished my degree, because let's face it, being unmarried and pregnant in hindsight was not the worst thing to happen to a person. It took years for me to connect with those feelings and my reactions to them.

When you feel shame and self-doubt, reasons to feel proud about yourself don't come naturally. I had no reason to believe I could achieve anything, and going back to school in my late 20s was such a leap of faith. And I did finally achieve my goal of graduating from university, in fact, I was pregnant with my fourth child during some of it, and it was just fine.

Being a single mother and raising my girls on my own for their early years, is the greatest achievement of my life. I loved it and wouldn't change a thing. Now I wear my singleton parenting badge with honour, but it took years to feel that way, and it didn't happen overnight. It took a series of events that changed my perception.

When I came back to Northern Ireland in 1992, I asked a friend, who ended up becoming my sister-in-law, if she was not embarrassed having a child without being married. We had children of a similar age and she looked me dead in the eye and said, "No, absolutely not." It sounded alien to me that she felt no shame. Was it growing up in different school systems or different countries? Was it what happened in the principal's office? I started to question why I felt differently about it.

If that had never happened, would I not have experienced feelings of shame at such a young age, when I had no control over it or the emotional intelligence to work through those feelings? Leaving university wouldn't have been the worst thing to happen; I may even have fought for my right to stay if I had some support. And being unmarried and pregnant didn't mean I had to wear a fake gold band on my wedding finger every time I went out.

The brain doesn't know the circumstances of the story, it just knows the feelings.

If I had never felt shame as a child, then would other moments of feeling shame not have been compounded? Trauma is not what happens to you, it's what happens within you.

Only through personal counselling, much later in life, did I finally get the chance to unpack all those feelings of shame. A good counselling session is like a hot bath; it stings at first but once the water has cooled and no one has pulled the plug, then the warmth of the water really can soothe the soul. Working through those feelings of shame, that were deep and having such an impact on my young adult life, was the only way I could finally move forward.

A chance conversation with my father, one night outside a service station, changed everything. I had often worked out in my head how I would apologise to him for letting him down, having had to leave university, but I didn't have the confidence to say it. Despite practising the apology many times in my head, I just couldn't get the words out.

But this night, I just blurted it out. "I'm sorry I disappointed you and let you down." He looked at me and said, "Ali, I couldn't be more proud of you. You're one of my greatest achievements. Look what you have achieved when all the odds were against you."

That was it in a nutshell. The shame I felt for all those years was an internal reference, one that had been opposed on me. It was certainly not how others saw me, yet I was allowing it to hold me back. I had no confidence that I could achieve much, despite knowing deep down inside, that I had the tools to do it. I worried so much about failure that I never even tried.

Once I let shame go, I was unstoppable. I applied for a new job, worked hard and got promoted. I said yes to everything I could to further my career. I listened and learnt, and studied as much as I could and slowly my confidence grew.

I came to Northern Ireland with the twins a little else. I met my husband the night I landed, although of course, we didn't know it then. Together, we grew a life, and strangely that was the easy bit. The hard bit was letting go of what was holding me back, and it wasn't success I was seeking, it was peace from the shame. Allowing myself to try and fail and knowing that the sky would not come crashing down.

When I started to tell my story and spoke of my feelings of shame to others who were compassionate, it lost its power. I would search my counsellors' face for disgust and it just wasn't there. I would search the faces of friends and colleagues in work and even strangers … and nothing. In fact, the reaction was usually one of awe and amazement that I had managed so well with twins, at such a young age. The more I talked about it, the more I accepted that the feelings of shame were not mine, I wasn't actually ashamed at all and I started to let them go.

It was so freeing to finally let it go. It was no longer triggering me in a way that was debilitating.

Unconscious triggers tend to be so impactful that we don't even know why we are responding in the way we are. According to Dr Gabor Mate, an emotional upset triggers the release of adrenaline and activates the sympathetic nervous system; our flight or fight component. When this happens, our bodies have little control over our feelings. I used to be triggered all the time and couldn't tell the story of my pregnancy, or my thoughts of suicide, because it was too upsetting, my body responding to an unconsciousness of previous feelings.

There is a difference between triggers ... and trips. I prefer to use the word *trips* now. Sometimes I still feel it and it trips me up, but because I am no longer governed by feelings of shame, I now recognise it for what it is. It's just a memory of a time when I didn't feel worthy. I still cry on the odd occasion and get upset, even after all these years, but it's just remembering the pain ... and that's okay. It's okay to be sad because it was a difficult time, and I can't take away the memory of how tough it was.

I had never told anyone about my thoughts of suicide; not then and not now. My circumstances improved, and the thoughts left me. The twins were born and my life changed forever in a good way and I can honestly say I have never had thoughts of suicide since. Working in suicide prevention has helped me to understand the concept of *Suicide Ideations* which can increase and decrease over a period of time, some-times even within hours. That's why it's so important to have as many people as possible, trained on how to have an effective suicide interven-tion conversation. As there is no 'typical' suicidal person and there is no 'typical' suicidal thought or idea, dismissing someone's thoughts as *that's not enough of a reason to die,* is unhelpful.

We are all at risk of reaching a point where we are so overwhelmed with our feelings and we reach the capacity to cope. Suicide is not about dying, it's about being unable to live with the emotional pain. Unfortunately, the brain doesn't know the difference. That's why, when we are heartbroken for example, we actually feel it physically.

When one of my daughters moved out of the house, I lay on the bed distraught and crying; I actually felt my heart *crack*. I told my husband who dismissed this with 'don't be silly, you're heart cant actually break.' I learnt later in life that extreme adrenalin surges can be caused by extreme stress. Takotsubo Cardiomyopathy, also known as broken heart syndrome, can occur when a person experiences severe emotional or physical distress. You can actually feel physical pain and it can be horrendous. If you were to break a leg, no one would expect you to manage that pain. It's treated with painkillers and supported in the way of a cast, but unfortunately there is no pill for emotional pain. We are expected to *just get on with it.*

Imagine a flower in your garden, and every year it bloomed so beautifully that the neighbours would talk about it. Now imagine if one year, it didn't bloom. You would do everything in your power to change the environment to support the flower. You might change the soil, give it shade, give it water and plant food, whatever was needed to support it. And I can guarantee, you would never blame the flower. But for some reason, as humans, when things go bad, we put the onus of responsibly onto ourselves - to make the change, to snap out of it. We are expected to reach out when we are at our most vulnerable and to fix whatever it is that has made us feel a certain way, but often it's the surrounding environment which has led us to struggle. You can't change what happens around you, you're not that powerful, but where you are more powerful, is not allowing what is happening around you to impact on your feelings. *No one* can make you feel a certain way.

I'm so grateful I didn't act on my thoughts of suicide. I look back on my life and my achievements and I'm truly proud of myself. However, my greatest achievement is that I am kind and compassionate, and work hard for others. Once I showed myself understanding and compassion and let go of the shame, I could apply this to others. The feelings I was carrying weren't serving me and were holding me back. One step at a time, one feeling at a time. I am a work in progress, but working through one feeling gave me the confidence to tackle another and then another, until the authentic belief in myself grew.

Remember, we are not our past, nor are we the feelings imposed upon us and recovery from suicide thoughts is possible

We only get to live this life journey once and I for one will be living mine proudly.

ALISON ARMSTRONG

A lison Armstrong was born in Northern Ireland and lives with her family in Lisburn. She spent a big part of her childhood in Birtley, Newcastle upon Tyne and her teens in Benoni, South Africa, bidding these sunny shores farewell in 1992 to return home to Northern Ireland after the birth of her twin daughters. She was subsequently married and has two sons and is also a grandmother.

A highly innovative, community focused and performance driven person, Alison has a wealth of experience in the alcohol, drug and suicide prevention remit and is currently the Director of Training & Development for the National Centre for Suicide Prevention Education & Training (NCSPET)

Alison has offered training in her above areas of expertise to various stakeholders, organisations and businesses primary across the UK but has ventured as far as Gibraltar, Bangkok, South Africa and India. Training and public speaking remains one of the most satisfying aspects of the work and she accredits her expertise to those she meets who bring a wealth of knowledge with them.

Alison has personally trained over 3000 people in Suicide Intervention Skills and believes that everyone should be trained in these skills thus reducing the stigma of suicide.

She also recently qualified as a celebrant - an avenue she never anticipated venturing into but one which has been extremely rewarding.

When she is not helping others through the diverse work she is involved in, Alison enjoys time with her family, a close circle of friends and empowering herself with knowledge, personally and professionally.

Alison's LinkedIn is www.linkedin.com/in/alison-armstrong-602850191/

LITTLE MISS PERFECT HAD A GREAT FALL
LISA BENSON

These days, if anyone were to call me a perfectionist, I would take it as an insult, not a compliment. What people are really saying is, *'You are inauthentic and can't connect with anyone else, let alone yourself.'* It has taken time for me to accept this new reality.

We interpret words from our experiences. I grew up thinking the word 'stop' was an unwanted setback. Stop signs and red lights were always inconvenient, breaking the momentum of my journey. I never valued rest. Any kind of stopping felt like a waste of time, and in a way, inefficient. My stomach churns as I'm reminded of a time in my life when I was forced to realise the value of being *stopped*.

'Thank you for sharing, Lisa.'

My writing mentor, Joanne, took a deep silent breath, honouring the piece I had read to the twelve other women in the circle. But to deflect my discomfort, I ripped a corner of the pretty wrapping paper covered notebook in which I'd written the words. *Please let me melt into the floor like the Wicked Witch of the West in* The Wizard of Oz.

It took all my strength to hold the tears in.

I was on a writing retreat in Fiji in 2016. We had formed a sacred ring of chairs and each of us had an opportunity to share what we'd written and receive feedback from a best-selling author – a rare opportunity for an amateur.

But while everyone else had bared their soul, I had read safe, empty words. I was choked up as the other women told deeply moving stories. Instead of sharing something vulnerable and meaningful I'd penned on the retreat, I read a piece I'd written before I arrived ... back when I was pretending to be unstoppable.

All my life, I'd gotten away with concealing the truth, but I couldn't get away with it here while maintaining an inauthentic façade. There was no way for me to only reveal the parts of my story that made me look good, as if it were a social media post – not if I was going to write an honest book about my life. I finally admitted in a middle-of-the-night-email to Joanne – after many private tears – that 'I need to be here the most.' Before the retreat, I figured I'd have my book published within a year. But the truth was, I'd have to start over.

This was the moment when I confronted my perfectionism, which had followed me like a shadow throughout my life. It had finally caught up with me. And it stopped me in my tracks.

As a young girl, I aspired to be just like my mum. I hadn't realised OCD (Obsessive Compulsive Disorder) behaviour wasn't the healthiest kind of modelling. I had always imagined everyone aimed for perfection. At school, I was called 'Little Miss Perfect' and was chuffed, even proud of the name. I was the epitome of flawlessness - a star student, immaculately groomed. I didn't know it at the time, but I was also delusional. Back then, I felt special and untouchable – somehow separated from the rest of humanity because of the way other people perceived me – someone who never had a hair out of place or ever made a mistake.

As I grew older and began to negotiate peer groups, work environments and dating, I began to feel the impact and far-reaching consequences of my perfectionism. I also grew up believing what others thought of me was of utmost importance, so I became a people pleaser. I was burdened with the double curse, which had me totally focused on external validation.

Because I did not speak up or offer my own opinions for fear of being disliked or not getting it right, I tended to just agree with whomever I was in conversation with. As a result, my own voice was buried somewhere unknown inside me. I put up with coercive, controlling relationships for over a decade because I was afraid to admit I'd failed in my choice of partner. I thought I was protecting the men in my life when I defended them from other people's unflattering comments, but the truth is, I was protecting myself from admitting I didn't have the perfect life.

When I was in my twenties, I left a job I'd enjoyed for three years. I resigned when I had to attend weekly sales meetings after a change to my role. I had to stand up and share my results in front of my colleagues. The first time it happened, I felt trapped inside my body as my hands sweated and my heart beat rapidly. It didn't take long for me to leave – because of my anxiety and having all eyes on me.

At every turn, I took the easy path to avoid failure or critique.

It was only during the five-year journey of writing my memoir that I began to understand the extent of how perfectionism had kept me small – and had stopped me from growing. The writing highlighted how much time I'd wasted. I shed many tears as I processed the reality of my life, while at the same time, I shed the weight of the shame and guilt I'd kept secret.

I have slowly allowed myself to peel away the layers of conditioning and become vulnerable. Being stopped dead at the retreat by my mentor, who didn't placate me or simply tell me what I wanted to hear, was instrumental in me finding the motivation to search for answers beneath my polished veneer. It allowed me to pause, while I looked with a new perspective at everything I had taken for granted. The journey has completely transformed my relationship with the word 'perfectionist.'

What I have come to see is that perfectionism is unattainable. It's an aspiration allowing us to procrastinate. It keeps us stuck so we don't have to expose our true selves and invite criticism or judgement. Perfectionists avoid this at all costs, unaware we are self-sabotaging. Trying to be perfect prevents us from ever feeling like we're 'good enough' because the goals are always just out of our reach. Although we fixate on the external (the way we look and how organised, immaculate or tidy we and our lives are), nothing we do helps resolve our deep dissatisfaction with our internal world, and a non-acceptance of self.

For a perfectionist, being 'unstoppable' is loaded with similar connotations - it describes someone who has achieved one hundred percent success, is invincible and almost surreal in their ability to perform, without making mistakes or experiencing setbacks. Of course, I rationally knew that this was absurd. Still, I'd always hoped to be a superwoman, magnificently unstoppable. However, whenever I fell short of my own standards, I felt more and more unworthy... *Perfectionist, unstoppable, superwoman.*

I have always felt the pressure to perform for the approval of others and been burdened by the expectation of single-handedly living up to any of these titles. I know I am not alone. These expectations take their toll on us physically, energetically and emotionally, as we try to prove we are worthy while we beat ourselves up for not being able to do 'it all.' Ironically, this creates a cycle of low, not high, self-esteem.

My painful experience at the writing retreat was a powerful wake-up call. I realised I wasn't as close to becoming an author as I'd imagined. I was stopped in my tracks. And in that place of being halted, the universe gave me space to expand my knowledge, so I could move forward, but in a healthier direction. I had to emotionally experience the story I was writing about, but with greater self-compassion and less self-judgement. This was the only way I could complete the dream to write my memoir. I had to write the book *I* needed to read. Here is where I learned that in the moments when we are stopped unexpectedly, the greatest transformations take place. These are the turning points that change us and define who we will become.

Like the Japanese art of kintsugi, my spirit was broken down and woven back together with the magic gold threads of learning, that helped me grow. In the process, I realised we all experience disruptions in our life. I found value and strength from honouring my scars.

With the increased focus on mental health in public discourse, I feel it necessary to debunk the myth that some people are just born unstoppable and everyone else is unworthy or deficient in some way. We can all feel unstoppable. It is the result of building momentum over time. Often, we compare ourselves with those who have spent years or decades working towards the 'roll' they are on. We judge our beginner self against someone else's advanced version. They may appear confident and polished, but we don't always see the struggle, mistakes or the long periods of stagnation they've also endured to get to where they are. Perhaps being unstoppable is more about persistence than perfection.

This too shall pass. I originally heard these words from the late Wayne Dyer, an internationally renowned self-development author and speaker. Every phase we go through in our lives … will pass. The good times won't continue forever, just as the tough days will come to an end, making way for the next lessons on our journey of transformation.

As we mature, we learn to accept the rhythm of positive and negative periods. It is my belief that no matter what is occurring, there is a higher reason which we don't always appreciate at the time. When everything feels dark, we can trust that the light days will return. I have found that when I share my challenging experiences (the ones that make me 'imperfect'), it offers comfort and hope to others who have forgotten that nothing in life is static. Everything changes. When I feel at my lowest ebb, I remember that everyone else also goes through times of suffering. Being labelled 'Little Miss Perfect,' did not exempt me from experiencing times of low emotional vibration. I too have wanted to give up, not knowing where to turn. These are universal human emotions which connect me to others. The irony is that it's not our successes that create emotional connection – these often create jealousies and comparisons. It's when we share our mistakes and vulnerabilities that we build bridges and inspire others.

We also tend to imagine that unstoppable people do it all alone, without any help. We regard success as a personal achievement. Our culture rewards and applauds individual, rapid success, as if it had nothing to do with family, community or environment. When, in history did our focus shift from valuing the individual over the community?

I am a co-author of an anthololgy called *Ubuntu – On Whose Shoulders We Stand*, compiled by Dr Tererai Trent. In my chapter, I acknowledge those who supported me to write and publish my memoir, *Where Have I Been All My Life?* (2022). I am forever grateful to my mentor and editor, publisher, husband, friends, family and many other supporters, without whom, I would have not been able to birth a book into the world.

There are always others around us, holding our hands to help us shine. We cannot get through life on our own. I believe these genuine connections are the backbone of humanity, allowing individuals to achieve success.

Without support we can't be unstoppable. We become unstoppable when we invest in our mental health and self-development. That is where we discover the pitfalls of perfectionism and the joy of failing and rebuilding ourselves anew.

In her book *Wifedom*, about the author George Orwell, Anna Funder exposes how George's wife, Eileen had a massive impact on his success. She was the invisible strength behind him. Her support and input remained unrecognised until Anna Funder brought her story into the light.

Since writing my memoir, and letting go of perfectionism, I have developed a different relationship with *being unstoppable.*

I now see it as resilience to external forces and being consistently brave enough to push though, even when I am scared or uncomfortable. I understand it as the relentless pursuit of authenticity, while still honouring the times when it's more productive for me to stop. I no longer judge myself harshly for having not having an 'always on' switch. For me, it is a dance that allows me to reflect and expand before the next burst of unstoppability. Even when we are unproductive, we can accept the pause as part of the ebb and flow of life.

My greatest insight is that we can always choose to have an unstoppable attitude.

Being unstoppable is not a title bestowed on us by others. It's not an unchosen label like 'Little Miss Perfect.' Unstoppable is a feeling. The feeling may start as a tiny seed of self-belief - we have to start somewhere. Growth occurs as a result of conviction. When we eyeball ourselves in the mirror and are proud of our bravery for making a difference, we gain internal momentum. The feeling becomes stronger when we realise we are not holding anything back through fear and are on a path that feels aligned with our unique purpose. The smallest breakthrough can be one tiny step towards a huge accomplishment.

My life changed, not when my life circumstances improved, or I became 'good enough,' but when I discarded my limiting beliefs. Our thoughts stop us. We may never meet the most unstoppable version of ourselves because we lack motivation or are faced with difficult life challenges. Sometimes we are stopped by uncontrollable events, like the pandemic. Other people, parents, partners, or our 'situation' can feel like obstacles – and we may even blame them and take on a victim narrative – but often, and in my case, I initiated my greatest pain. Yes, I feared failure, but I also feared success. I eventually realised my self-imposed limiting beliefs were blocking me from being the most powerful version of myself. I wasted so much time trying to live up to labels instead of being me.

In my experience, perfectionism stops us from being unstoppable. I know it because I've been there. When we are living to please others, we cannot be authentic. And who would want to be unstoppably inauthentic? Once I let go of all the trying, and nurtured my unique gifts, I was free to soar.

In the year following the publication of my book, I co-authored four anthologies, wrote a guest contribution for *The Freedom in Forgiveness* by Karen Weaver, won five book awards for my memoir, was a finalist in the Woman Changing the World and Roar Awards and my book was included in the Hollywood Swag Bag gifted to all Oscar nominees. My memoir was translated into Czech for a women's congress in The Czech Republic and Slovakia. I was a guest on numerous podcasts and interviews. I gave a number of speeches and attended the Serenity Press Crom Castle Retreat in Ireland where I spoke on an international stage about my own book and as part of a launch of some anthologies. I connected with authors and speakers and met Sarah, Duchess of York and Dr Tererai Trent who is Oprah's favourite guest of all time.

It all feels surreal.

I could have given up multiple times, but I instinctively knew the hard way was essential for my development. I would never have had these opportunities if I hadn't taken the first difficult step on a journey of many years of internal work and writing. I had to build up the courage to share my story.

In November 2023, I spoke at the Serenity Press Writer's Retreat at Crom Castle about how perfectionists cannot be authentic. I had no notes and no prompts. I took deep breaths to calm my heart rate as I waited my turn, but as soon as I took hold of the microphone, my body loosened. I forgot several points I had planned on sharing, but it didn't matter. It wasn't 'perfect,' but it was heartfelt and authentic.

In the past, my fears would have won. Even a few years ago, I wouldn't have been able to expose myself to potential criticism. Although I was nervous, my purpose outweighed my fear of failure or what anyone might think. We feel unstoppable when we know that what we are doing is greater than us and in service of others.

Afterwards, several women approached me to say my words resonated deeply with them. One said, 'That hit me hard.'

We initiate transformation, when we show up before we feel ready. Others may be relying on us to have a voice, which in turn helps them gain the courage to use their own.

When I let go of resistance, I had a chance to become resilient. When I stopped trying to be accepted or liked by others and put the effort into working on myself, I gave myself the opportunity to shine.

It doesn't matter that the road ahead of me will be crooked, all that matters is it's mine. *Aaaah*. I feel the release of a long, expansive breath as I type these words. Finally, I have a sense of freedom, knowing I don't need anyone's approval to follow a particular path as long as I value my own opinion. That's what makes me feel unstoppable. I thought achieving perfection was the key to success, but it turns out this belief was the very obstacle standing in my way.

LISA BENSON

L isa Benson is a self-diagnosed recovering perfectionist who spent five years writing her multi-award winning memoir, *Where Have I Been All My Life?* During this time, she lived part time on a boat on Sydney Harbour which she found to be a peaceful and inspirational space for her writing. Lisa and her husband continue to lead a 'double life' travelling between Newcastle and Sydney each week.

Lisa has a Bachelor of Business Degree with a major in tourism and marketing. She previously held various sales and marketing positions in hotels and resorts, and also worked in a real estate office. It wasn't until Lisa was in her forties that she decided to pursue her lifelong dream of becoming an author, and she now writes full-time.

Lisa's motto is *Stop Trying – Start Being* although she spent most of her life doing the exact opposite. Her writing is honest and relatable, and she hopes her vulnerability helps others feel less alone. Lisa would love to inspire women to stop wasting time living up to other people's expectations, to discover the magic of living an authentic life and to be free of self-imposed limitations.

If you would like to hear more from Lisa, you can follow her on Instagram (lisabensonauthor), Facebook (Lisa Benson Author) or LinkedIn (Lisa Benson).

Lisa's website is www.lisabensonauthor.com

I AM A MIDWIFE
NADINE ROBINSON

ONE

I leap from bed, heart pounding, scrambling for what has broken my precious sleep.

"Hello, it's Nadine," I whisper into the phone, creeping out of the bedroom so as not to wake my husband. Patiently listening.

Contractions, waters, blood.

Pulling on clothes, hopping on one foot, sweeping my hair back into a ponytail, I crash into the kitchen, gathering the drugs that must be kept refrigerated, keys, my phone charger … and water. I thrust myself out the door into the crisp night air; alone, steady, heightened.

Arrival at the home yields candles and flickering darkness.

Gingerly, I enter the space, feeling, assessing, intuiting.

The humus smell of blood greets my nose. A hedonic growl escapes the fierce woman on the floor on hands and knees; naked, carelessly wild.

Gleaming fluids drip between her legs; steady, a promise.

I move so as not to disturb the silent slumber, the tender strength of rest between these powerful waves.

Mama's head, drooping, her breath, bedrock.

The baby; demanding, stretching skin taut as we listen to the haunting rhythm of life.

The piercing gaze of peak pain, staunch, as another towering wave crests. The tang is unrepentantly pungent. The lowing moves from the chest, down to the grotto of life bulging with slick glistening, matted hair, stringy fluids and blood. With a groan, her hand moves to cradle this silky head within her most tender of flesh.

The skull emerges, leisurely, ears unfurl, nape of neck.

The full head of hair hastily recoils, as if to return to its secret enclave.

The pause.

That brief moment between amorphous life and landing. Babe's eyes closed.

Unaware?

Patient.

The uterus stands tall, preparing for its final expeditious task.

The newly born head twists and the body oozes from its cosmic shroud, slithery and sinuous.

A primal howl of awe and release, as dad, hands under mine, lifts this new being to the earth of mama's breasts, looping, once, twice, a flourish of braided cord from baby's neck.

Tears drip, raining kisses, opening to the breath of life.

That's how I felt about midwifery. It was the most magical, most perfect thing in the world.

TWO

I sat hunched on the toilet, crying in agony as knives slashed through my bladder. I was begging the Gods that my pager wouldn't go off. I heard the dreaded beep. Of course it did. I crawled out of the bathroom and packed up, sick and in pain, off to attend another birth.

This is how my almost 20-year midwifery career ended; crying on the toilet. It wasn't splashy or snazzy or honourable. It was shameful. I was a burnout failure who couldn't do my job.

So, what does a washed-up midwife do with her career? I had devoted my entire life to midwifery. Catching babies is not a transferable skill. I had invested tens of thousands of dollars, travelled the world and expected I would grow old teaching women how to midwife their communities.

My children's upbringing was woven into the fabric of birth. I home-schooled my 4 daughters. We made clay models of vulvas and talked about periods for science class. I breastfed for 14 years in total, slept with my babies, treated colds with herbs and caught babies underwater.

I was an edgy, crunchy, homebirth, homeschooling midwife.

Peace on earth begins with birth. - Jeannine Pavarti Baker

Midwifery is a gruelling career. We make life or death decisions every day. We usually work alone, with long shifts on call, and often in conflict with physicians and nurses.

If I wasn't a homebirth, hippie midwife … who the hell was I?

THREE

Midwifery is a calling. It's not a job. It's not a career. It's certainly not a profession.

There is a passion that burns. It's so fierce that once it's been lit, it's almost impossible to extinguish.

It's a surrender to being the guardian that stands between the cosmic realities of life and death, knowing we are often helpless.

Midwives walk with the veiled secrets of birth, of women, of blood.

I will never forget the wonder, the excitement and the utter, "holy fuck this is the most magnificent thing I have every experienced," feeling when I did my first four-handed catch with the midwife who was train-ing me. It was a freezing November night. The stars were shards of glass, twinkling to welcome this baby. It felt secret and special and wondrous. I walked into the house; a beautiful mama on her hands and knees in the living room. It was calm, peaceful. I quietly went about setting up birth equipment. It is the apprentice midwife's job to set up and clean up. I have scrubbed out hundreds of birth pools.

The midwives did the charting and clinical assessments, but mostly we stayed out of the way so the birthing mama could weave her magic. I sat back on my hands, just witnessing. I had attended home births before, but this was something different. I wasn't just witnessing; I was testing my knowing and intuition.

I asked myself: "How many centimetres dilated do I think she is, based on how she's acting?" "Are the towels in the dryer?" "Does the mama need a backrub? A sip of water? Should the lights be different?"

"Where are the drugs, the O2 and the Doppler [ultrasound] in case we need to provide clinical intervention?"

The midwives were hands off, meaning they trusted and believed in birth. Heck ... I figured birth just works! I had attended about fifty births at this point and most of the time it did. The mama was perfect. She knew exactly what she was doing. Suddenly the energy in the room shifted and she started to push. I peeked down...

FOUR

When I quit midwifery, I cried for a year.

I sat, hours on end, hunched over on the floor of my office, questioning everything. Everything I believed about myself was shattered. My husband made a good living. Could I just cook, travel and be a happy housewife?

I was desperate and tried to find a career that would utilise my midwifery skills. I remember weeping with relief after I signed up for a Dancing for Birth training. I wildly thought I could walk "near" midwifery. I was panicked, thinking, somehow, I could salvage the shreds of my midwifery career.

I'm a 6/2 manifestor, with a Pisces sun, Scorpio rising and a Capricorn moon. I am a visionary disruptor. I have to be in ... up to my eyeballs, radically devoted, passionately devoured by my work. And I had to throw it ALL away.

I quit being a clinical director of midwifery.

I stopped examining new midwives.

I sold my midwifery practice.

I was no longer catching babies.

I had to burn it all down.

Midwifery is a little bit like a bad ex; you're always making excuses for the shitty parts and somehow, they sneakily pull you back in…maybe we can make it work like this?

Nothing about this was simple or easy. I had no examples of women who were doing what I was doing at 40 years old. I had no idea if there was a career on the other side of midwifery.

So, I bundled up my soft skills - sexual health and education, spirituality, birth, death, couples counselling, and holistic healing – and repackaged myself as a healer.

It was confusing. I felt like a fish out of water. I started charging *gasp* $75 an hour! I limped along, seeing a few people a month. It felt like an expensive hobby. Most years, I spent more money on essential oils, books and training than I ever made in my business.

My marriage was better. My children were happier. But I was still crumbling inside.

As a woman who did meaningful, life changing work with other women, could I really be satisfied with this quasi-professional business that nobody really knew about?

FIVE

I miss the rawness of midwifery.

I miss the surprises and the secrets that are revealed.

I miss the clients who chose midwifery as a way of life, not because it was trendy.

I miss three-year payment plans where we would see our clients every month as they dropped off $50 to pay for their birth. We were never shortchanged by a client.

I miss walking with women in their darkest moments and witnessing them stand on the other side of birth; powerful, unstoppable, free.

I miss supporting women to have their breech babies at home, underwater.

I miss the blood and the unrefined earthiness of the body.

I miss coming home and having hot, oxytocin-fueled sex with my husband after a delicious and undisturbed homebirth.

I don't miss being on call.

I don't miss epidurals.

I don't miss doctors and nurses whispering about me and my clients as I walk by the desk.

I don't miss 11pm pages from clients who suddenly make time to call because they've had a cold for three days.

I don't miss hollering, "We'll finish talking when I get home!" to the sad faces of my daughters as I left them, running to a birth

I don't miss bringing two cars everywhere we went, just in case.

I don't miss being absent for Christmases, birthdays and special occasions.

I don't miss sobbing on my bed after catching a baby who was born still.

SIX

I can honestly say I haven't quite found the same passion, the same bliss, the same all-consuming enthusiasm I had for midwifery.

But maybe that's a good thing?

Midwifery, sort of, eats you alive from the inside out. It's like a parasite - always demanding more. More to learn, more to do, more to chart, more to practise.

The rewards are magnificent. The costs are heavy.

And yet the work I do now is entirely informed by midwifery:

The client is the expert

Sex is foundational to your entire well-being

Have you looked at your vagina today? ☒

Working as a healer and coach is incredible. Yet even as I write this, my heart is pounding, I have tears in my eyes and I can feel how important that work was.

Midwifery was one of my highest highs and quitting it was my Dark Night of the Soul.

The effects still linger.

I am happier.

I am more grounded.

I am a better mother and wife.

But I'm not yet sure I am a better me.

Breaking up with your heart's desire and soul's work is never easy. But it shouldn't be, should it?

I think I would question everything about myself if I didn't ache like this.

I think I would be tempted to get sucked back into this work if I hadn't paid the ultimate cost: my health.

My bladder still acts up on occasion. Stabbing pains and burning creep in to remind me you're over stretched, you need more sleep, what the heck are you doing now?

I devoted an entire year to healing my bladder, eating well and working on the emotional aspects of my illness.

The emotional question of the bladder? Who are you pissed off at?

There was an answer here I wasn't quite ready to admit to.

The technical diagnosis of my bladder condition is called "interstitial cystitis"

"Interstitial cystitis, a type of bladder pain syndrome, is chronic pain in the bladder and pelvic floor of unknown cause. It is the urologic chronic pelvic pain syndrome of women. Symptoms include feeling the need to urinate right away, needing to urinate often, and pain with sex. IC/BPS is associated with depression and lower quality of life." 1

Most women never get better from IC. Treatment is often about managing symptoms and hoping you don't get worse. I can take care of myself now in a way I never could as a midwife; I read more, I eat well, I sleep through the night. And ... I can keep my bladder happy.

My life is rich and woven through with spirituality, travel to exotic places, soul conversations, ceremonies in the forest, firewalking, mind-blowing sex with my husband, sitting naked on the beach, and adventures with our grandbabies.

It's delicious. It's passionate and full. And yet, I still yearn for the intensity of midwifery. The yearning helps me with remembering all that was good and special and wise about midwifing, women and birth.

Walking the path as a healer is never easy. It's fraught with challenges, difficulties, pain and suffering. It's listening to people, hearing their stories and witnessing their pain. It's learning lessons (sometimes the hard way) and knowing you can't always fix things.

The fullness of my sorrow reminds me that I was good. Really good. Sometimes even exceptional. Keeping that version of myself in my mind's eye helps me to explore more deeply who I am.

I am a proud wife, with an incredible husband. I am a devoted friend, who has deep and fulfilling relationships with two best friends, both of whom I met through midwifery. I am a daughter, sister and aunt. I am a loving mother and grandmother, who never has to miss another Christmas.

I am a phoenix reborn from the fires and blood of birth. The agonies I witnessed, the stories of sexual trespass and learning the secrets of women's bodies have allowed me to become an exceptional healer.

I am a midwife.

---

1 Wikipedia Accessed Dec 3, 2021 https://en.wikipedia.org/wiki/Interstitial_cystitis

NADINE ROBINSON

Nadine Robinson is a revolutionary holistic women's health and relationships expert who has worked with thousands of clients across the globe. Her clients have been able to successfully heal chronic illnesses, overcome romantic problems like infidelity and even build nine-figure businesses.

Nadine brings to her clients two decades of experience as a midwife as well as certifications in firewalking and other holistic health practices. Her expertise has been featured in the media including the Huffington Post. Daily Blast Live, Medium and more.

She is the international bestselling author of The Holistic Entrepreneur: Creating Success with the Medicine of your Soul.

Nadine lives in Calgary, Alberta, Canada, but spends her summers at an island home where she frolics on the naked beach. She is blissfully married to the man of her dreams and is a grandmother to three.

Nadine's website is www.nadinerobinson.com

GERALDINE MCGRATH

Creating meaningful connections with incredible individuals like yourself is my calling. My unique gift lies in guiding people to uncover and embrace their inner strength, enchantment, and unstoppable version.

Should you choose to embark on a journey to unlock the Unstoppable you, I am here to offer my support.

Whether it's through personalised one-on-one sessions or within the dynamic setting of my group programmes, I'm dedicated to assisting you in this transformation.

To learn more and discover the path that suits you best, kindly indicate your interest below. I will make it a point to reach out to you personally.

Create a connection or explore future collaborations with me.

Listen to my Award Winning Podcast
Radiate Realness

Discover more of Geraldine's
Journey, scan below.

Dare to be Unstoppable; it all lies within,
-Geraldine McGrath

Milton Keynes UK
Ingram Content Group UK Ltd.
UKHW041057260224
438492UK00006B/425